Elevating Marginalized Voices in Academe: Lessons for a New Generation of Scholars centers and amplifies the narratives that will transform the future of academia. These narratives invite the exchange of ideas and the sharing of lived experiences from Black, Indigenous and Latin* people. By challenging the romanticization of traditional scholarship, this text will open the readers' minds and hearts to the courageous moments documented in its pages.

Cristobal Salinas Jr., PhD, Associate Professor, Florida Atlantic University; Founder and Editor-in-Chief, Journal Committed to Social Change on Race and Ethnicity

Storytelling is powerful. The stories in this book provide heartfelt anecdotes of doctoral student experiences in the Academy. The book is a good reminder for doctoral students that they are not alone, that their work is valued, and that what they are doing in their program is indeed needed. For students needing that extra push while earning their degree, please read as affirmation that you belong and you matter.

Evette L. Allen Moore, PhD, Executive Director, Multicultural Affair & Inclusive Excellence, Arkansas State University

This book is a gift that offers rich insights from a diverse array of scholars of color who have recently traversed the academy. Many of the narratives highlight promising practices for future graduate students of color or for those striving to support them. Readers will find advice for building one's doctoral committee, cultivating community, processing criticism, and saving space for self-care. This book is a love letter in which aspiring graduate students of color will find wisdom, penned with care and bravery; secrets that often go untold for fear of repercussion; and encouragement to always seek joy and know you belong.

Leslie D. Gonzales, EdD, Associate Professor, Department of Educational Administration, Faculty Excellence Advocate, Michigan State University

Elevating Marginalized Voices in Academe

This book shares advice, how-to's, validations, and cautionary tales based on minoritized students' recent experiences in doctoral studies. Providing a change of view from inspirational works framed at the "traditional" graduate student towards the affirmation of marginalized voices, readers are given a look at the multiplicitous experiences of underrepresented identities in the predominantly, and historically, White academy. With the changing landscape of America's institutions of higher education, this book shares tools for navigating spaces intended for the elite. From the personal to professional, these words of wisdom and encouragement are useful anecdotes that speak to the practitioner and academic.

Emerald Templeton, EdD is a community college administrator and assistant professor with a background in higher education, student affairs, and counseling student development. Her research interests are emerging in two areas of work: the logic of valuing diversity and Black women in higher education.

Bridget H. Love, EdD is an administrator in a local government agency, and a community college professor with a background in government, community corrections, and higher education. Her cross-disciplinary research interests center on the questions, "Who is telling the story? and What is being said? as a way to curate and custodian the experiences of Black women.

Onda Johnson, EdD is a government administrator in public policy for k-12 education. Johnson spent her career serving youth in institutional and educational settings. Her research interests span early childhood development and leadership in Pre-k-12 learning environments and the derivatives of social justice in educational spaces.

Elevating Marginalized Voices in Academe

Lessons for a New Generation
of Scholars

**Edited by Emerald Templeton,
Bridget H. Love, and Onda Johnson**

Routledge
Taylor & Francis Group

NEW YORK AND LONDON

First published 2021
by Routledge
52 Vanderbilt Avenue, New York, NY 10017

and by Routledge
2 Park Square, Milton Park, Abingdon, Oxon, OX14 4RN

Routledge is an imprint of the Taylor & Francis Group, an informa business

Library of Congress Cataloging-in-Publication Data
Names: Templeton, Emerald, editor. | Love, Bridget H., editor. | Johnson, Onda, editor.
Title: Elevating marginalized voices in academe: lessons for a new generation of scholars/edited by Emerald Templeton, Bridget H. Love, Onda Johnson.
Description: New York, NY: Routledge, 2021. | Includes bibliographical references and index.
Identifiers: LCCN 2020042558 (print) | LCCN 2020042559 (ebook) | ISBN 9780367490713 (hardback) | ISBN 9781003044338 (ebook)
Subjects: LCSH: Minority graduate students—United States—Anecdotes. | Doctoral students—United States—Anecdotes. | Minority graduate students—Vocational guidance—United States. | Doctoral students—Vocational guidance—United States. | Minority graduate students—United States—Social conditions.
Classification: LCC LB2371.4.E54 2021 (print) | LCC LB2371.4 (ebook) | DDC 378.1/550973—dc23
LC record available at https://lccn.loc.gov/2020042558
LC ebook record available at https://lccn.loc.gov/2020042559

ISBN: 9780367490713 (hbk)
ISBN: 9780367490720 (pbk)
ISBN: 9781003044338 (ebk)

Typeset in ITC New Baskerville Std by KnowledgeWorks Global Ltd.

Dedication

This work was one of the heart, mind, and hands. With our collective experiences, we commit to elevating the voices of the marginalized and honoring the narratives of scholars of color. In turn, we dedicate this project to

- those who have gone before us because they have laid the foundation upon which we stand and continue to move forward;
- those who are on the path and stand shoulder to shoulder as we work in solidarity towards justice; and
- those who are to come. For you are the future, and you carry the burden of the past yet the hope of many.

Contents

Acknowledgments

We humbly acknowledge the voices not spoken through this text, not heard in the academy, ignored in society, and filtered through all forms of media. Our eyes, ears, and hearts are open and ready to receive what you impart. We thank our editorial team, Matthew Friberg and Jessica Cooke, for their excitement in and commitment to bringing this work to the world.

Foreword: On Belonging to Liberation

Uma Mazyck Jayakumar, PhD
University of California at Riverside

This forward is a love letter to those voices of doctoral students of color who least fit in and feel othered in the academy. To those for whom this book is written: You represent the greatest hope for an antiracist institution. As a scholar who did not fit in as a doctoral student and has now "made it" I also want to warn that when your existence and the stance you proactively take to be an advocate is a threat to the system, this institution will certainly continue to try to make you feel unwelcome. But that is exactly why you do belong— you belong when it comes to a vision toward liberation. I and we must begin to recognize these exclusionary attempts as a signal of our tremendous worth and purpose in academia and beyond. Remember that you and I represent those more worthy who are not yet here. Fill the room (of otherwise mostly White administrators or uncritical folks) with those faces, opinions and voices that you know deserve to be in that room but are excluded by design. Those individuals—that imagined liberatory space—are to whom and where we should ever strive to belong. What would they be saying, what would they be asking of you, what can you do now with your educational privilege to do right by the community to which you have an allegiance (not the one in your presence)? These are the questions that must remain top of mind, these are the folks we must remain accountable to. Because trust that when you are in that meeting where racism needs to be called out, where a policy or practice with negative consequences needs to be fought against, you may continue to be the only one that stands up, that speaks out. Your White colleagues may thank you during (but it's usually after) for your comments, while remaining silent on the matter themselves. You will see who—White and of color—is (and who is not) willing to do the work, to risk their own comfort. Comparing yourself to others in that room, starting to better "fit in," is not something to strive for.

Be strategic, but always stay true to yourself and a broader vision for racial justice.

Reading this text reminded me of so many instances in graduate school that I had not thought about in years. A faculty in my program told me I did not belong in graduate school because I didn't know what I wanted to study. It was only years later that I would be able to see the common theme across my "undefinable interests" as focused on racial climate and racial justice praxis. That same faculty would come up to me after I received a dissertation of the year award, to share his genuine shock that I received the same award he had years prior (meant as a compliment). I was not often the first or even last student thought of when funding opportunities arose so I had to volunteer on projects or seek external support and funding. Finding my people, across the school of education and across institutions was key. They and the advisor (who came to my department in my third year) that I eventually graduated under were my guardian angels. How powerful it would have been to read this book as a doctoral student. I would have devoured it. Now those experiences and lessons allow me to persist in the face of being devalued for my contributions and advocacy efforts. Just last week, my colleagues voted against counting my 100-page Expert Report, written on behalf of student intervenors of color in an ongoing race-conscious affirmative action court case involving University of North Carolina (UNC), to support my merit review. While they could see a journal article written for a primarily academic audience as scholarship, their perspective steeped in whiteness did not allow for the acknowledgement of the type of impactful writing we should be doing more often as scholars. As brilliantly articulated in this book, it is so important that we define for ourselves who we are in academic spaces.

The second point I want to touch on is survival. More importantly, it is going beyond survival toward healing. As bell hooks states, "I came to theory because I was hurting—the pain within me was so intense that I could not go on living. I came to theory desperate, wanting to comprehend—to grasp what was happening around and within me. Most importantly, I wanted to make the hurt go away." Quite often the fight for liberation within systems of oppression, parallels an internal fight to liberate and heal ourselves from personal and institutional trauma. We might be drawn toward fighting institutional racism alongside oppressed communities we are a part of and care about, as part of a process that can eventually include a personal liberation project. Jeanine Staples' groundbreaking work on emotional justice is helpful for lighting the way (see thesupremeloveproject.com).

Many of us entered the academic waters on a similar journey, but later found it necessary to focus on not drowning. Yet we grow our capacity to come up for air and even embrace the joy and beauty of what is also an enveloping ocean of possibility. This book exemplifies a path to survival and healing. The authors, voices, more than mine, offer guidance on the how. The narratives bravely expressed here constitute a validating and welcoming counter space for all not otherwise seen by the academy. Each chapter provides a window into an experience the academy and dominant narratives like to tuck away and hide. Each author makes visible the types of experiences that signal hope for a liberatory education, by sharing tips, tools of resistance, and navigational strategies, and by virtue of their presence in an otherwise White supremecist, patriarchal, anti-Black space.

The last thing I'll say is an acknowledgment, to the "othered" doctoral students and communities that teach me every day, that inspire me to think more critically, that motivate me to advocate and fight within my own institution and within an exceedingly frustrating and limiting White supremacist legal system. To the people I imagine in every room I walk into—whether a faculty meeting, a university-wide admissions committee, or a court case shaping the fate of race-conscious affirmative action—to the people writing in this volume, to the editors of this book who took my class years ago, and to those for whom this volume is written, thank you from the depths of my heart.

Preface

Purpose

Elevating Marginalized Voices in Academe: Letters to a New Generation of Scholars fulfills a critical gap in the literature about marginalized identities in the academy. This work stems from our own experiences in searching for useful texts and resources that described, supported, and recognized the experiences students of color face throughout doctoral studies. Existing literature often highlights the challenges of faculty of color pursuing the tenure track, or students of color in general. However, the persistent theme of exclusion through all levels of academia alongside the distinct expectations within doctoral education, set this book apart from others. Countering the narratives of the "traditional" graduate student, this text serves to affirm and center the marginalized voices that are ever present and changing how higher education and scholarship look today.

This anthology of narratives gives readers a look at the multiplicitous experiences of underrepresented identities in the predominantly, and historically, White academy. With the changing landscape of America's institutions of higher education, the writers share tools for navigating spaces that were intended for the elite. From the personal, to academic, and professional, these words of wisdom and encouragement are useful anecdotes that speak to the practitioner and academic. A text aimed at uncovering the unknown and unspoken in traversing doctoral studies, this work is an insightful, critical, and true-to-heart read for the rising intellectual in coming to know their scholarly identity.

Audience

The intended audience for this book is current and future generations of scholars of color, their counterparts in the academy, and the academicians who hope to support them. For scholars of color, we hope that the variety of narratives and perspectives in this text will resonate with their own and demonstrate a sense of solidarity, hope, and grounding. For other scholars who are learning and working alongside scholars of color, we envision this book as a beacon for recognizing and understanding the differences in academic experiences, and a tool for true allyship. For academicians—faculty, administrators, and leaders in higher education—this text will serve as a resource for instituting programs, policies, and practices that support doctoral students of color through and out of their studies. Additionally, this text will be an excellent resource for introductory courses in doctoral programs across disciplines.

Organization of the Book

The introductory chapter of this book sets its tone by reviewing the history of silencing marginalized voices and the challenges of defining scholarships in a White space. By underscoring the need to confront the dominant narrative about *who* has rights to the academy and the production of scholarship, the Introduction leads with a call to uplift, center, and resound the voices of students of color.

This text includes three sections: Developing Scholarly Identity; Curating Community; and Race, Space, and Time. Each section is preceded by a brief introduction, which highlights the common themes and connections between the chapters in that section.

The first section, *Developing Scholarly Identity*, describes how the authors therein came to define scholarship and therefore developed their own scholarly identity. Describing their experiences navigating academic contexts, these authors share insight to the advancement of their intellectual thought and the centering of their narratives. The next section, *Curating Community*, chronicles the author's relational experiences forming, storming, and norming. From selecting, accepting, and engaging with various persons, the authors describe how their communities were curated. In addition, the authors share how these communities aided in their matriculation, strengthened their scholarly identities, and continue to spark their advocacy. The third and final section, *Race, Space, and Time*, envelopes the experiences of graduate students of color in predominantly White institutions. Authors recount their time in doctoral programs in racialized environments situated in marginalized positions. Under adverse conditions, students of color form ways of being that turn away from stereotyped expectations, and in doing so, promote changes that raise hope for the advancement of future graduate students of color.

Together, the three parts of this book cover a breadth of experiences and multifaceted narratives of students who have traditionally existed on the margins. Though this compilation of stories cannot possibly address the experiences of every person of color who has embarked upon doctoral studies, it is our sincere hope that this work begins to peel back the layers of territory not yet unearthed.

Introduction

Emerald Templeton, Bridget H. Love,
and Onda Johnson

> "The paradox of education is precisely this—that as one begins to become conscious one begins to examine the *society* in which he is being educated."
>
> — James Baldwin

The state of higher education in America has changed and continues to do so. The individuals populating today's college and university campuses are increasingly more diverse coming from various socio-economic, ethnoracial, political, intersectional, and global perspectives. Unlike times past, obtaining an advanced degree is becoming much more of a requirement than an opportunity to enrich one's life. In the past two decades, the percentage of individuals holding a master's degree or higher has almost doubled (National Center for Educational Statistics, n.d.). For people of color, rates of attendance in institutions of higher education are rapidly growing. This race for advancing education includes experiences that are disparate based on social identities. American higher education has been built upon a foundation of elitism—a dominant ideological front that suggests that the select are greater than the sum; and exclusion—the intentional act of barring access.

Background

Lessons is an anthology of narratives from scholars of color about traversing doctoral studies in American higher education. With each chapter representing a letter written to the increasingly demographically diverse students entering the academy, this edited volume will underscore experiences, challenges, how-to's, and validations from scholars of color who have navigated predominantly and historically

White institutions. This book of lessons provides a unique view into the academic lives of new scholars and challenges the idea of the "traditional" graduate student, and subsequently who is recognized as a scholar.

This project is important as it fulfills the call from extant literature to uplift the voices of marginalized people. In Aaron Kuntz's (2015) work on responsible methodology, he stresses the importance of truth-telling and risk taking in scholarly work by challenging the "who," "how," and "why" as well as the "what" in legitimizing scholarship. He carefully critiques the charge of the scholarly community to conduct scientific inquiry and suggests that such a focus on procedure misses out on the transformative power of scholarship. Scholars have "an ethical duty to tell critical truths" by "interrogating the normative means of coming to know," (Kuntz, p. 103). It is our intent to bolster the voices of people of color through this work and the ways in which they have come to know what it means to be a scholar in an elite academy that was not meant for them. While this book is not empirically-based in format or style, the essence of its contents is qualitative as we seek to uncover the thick, rich narratives that come by way of delving into the personal stories of trials, tribulations, and triumphs. As described by Kuntz, the power of unveiling these narratives is an intimate act situated between truth-telling and activism. To that end, *Lessons* demonstrates how "good qualitative inquiry does more than describe; it intervenes on multiple material levels" (Kuntz, 2015, p. 68).

Similarly, Hill-Collins' (2000) work on Black Feminist Thought highlights the need to center the voices of the marginalized in places where they've been silenced. She postulates that

> Oppressed groups are frequently placed in the situation of being listened to only if we frame our ideas in the language that is familiar to and comfortable for a dominant group. This requirement often changes the meaning of our ideas and works to elevate the ideas of dominant groups.
>
> (Hill-Collins, 2000, p. vii)

Our work serves to elevate the stories of people of color who have often navigated the throes of the academy in silence. In essence, this book is a way of reclaiming our voices and taking our rightful place within the scholarly community. Building upon Hill-Collins' ideas, *Lessons* showcases the expertise of recent doctoral candidates in the cultural knowledge and power they bring to scholarship through an accessible text.

We define the counter-story as a method of telling the stories of those people whose experiences are not often told (i.e., those on the margins of society). The counter-story is also a tool for exposing, analyzing, and challenging the majoritarian stories of racial privilege. Counter-stories can shatter complacency, challenge the dominant discourse on race, and further the struggle for racial reform.

(Solorzano & Yosso, 2002, p. 32)

Chapters are written in first person covering a broad range of experiences, advice, and insights from the writer's own encounters as a person of color in doctoral studies. The style of writing includes personal accounts, observations, and narratives including lessons learned and recommendations.

Framework for Uplifting Marginalized Voices

Nash (2004) pointedly highlighted the necessity for the personal narrative in scholarly works illuminating the rich meaning that could be gleaned and "when delivered well, can deliver to your readers those delicious aha! moments of self and social insight that are all too rare in more conventional forms of research" (p. 24). Similarly, Solorzano and Yosso (2002) underscore counter-storying as "a tool for exposing, analyzing, and challenging the majoritarian stories of racial privilege" (p. 32). In this book, the narratives of scholars of color are constructed within three themes: Developing Scholarly Identity, which broadly addresses defining one's own scholarship in the midst and sometimes in spite of the dominant narrative; Curating Community, which highlights the importance of connectedness and belonging; and Race, Space, and Time, which encompasses the tools and strategies used in navigating the academic environment. Using a personal narrative approach, the collection of chapters are grounded in the experiences of students of color throughout doctoral studies.

References

Hill-Collins, P. (2000). *Black feminist thought: Knowledge, consciousness, and the politics of empowerment.* New York: Routledge.

Kuntz, A. M. (2015). *The responsible methodologist: Inquiry, truth-telling, and social justice.* Walnut Creek, CA: Left Coast Press, Inc.

Nash, R. J. (2004). *Liberating scholarly writing: The power of personal narrative.* New York, NY: Teachers College Press.

National Center for Educational Statistics (n.d.). Fast Facts. Retrieved from: https://nces.ed.gov/fastfacts/display.asp?id=27

Solorzano, D. G., & Yosso, T. J. (2002). Critical race methodology: Counter-storytelling as an analytical framework for education research. *Qualitative Inquiry, 8*(1), 23–44.

Part I

Developing a Scholarly Identity

What is scholarship? Who defines it? Who has rights to it? Where does it exist? These are the questions that underlie feelings of doubt, Imposter Syndrome, Stereotype Threat, and Racial Battle Fatigue. It is not inconceivable that students and academics alike grapple with these questions, and further, attempt to define and describe scholarship within their own contexts. It is also plausible that students of color, for whom the academy has been affixed to systemic oppression and exclusion, are grappling with these questions in challenging and sometimes painful ways. Scholarship, often situated juxtaposed to academic rigor, is nuanced, contextual, and coded. Defining one's scholarly identity is seen as a process coupled with the execution of successful research and publication though access to these opportunities are not equitably distributed across racial lines.

The narratives in this text reveal the manifold layers of developing a scholarly identity during doctoral studies. Navigating dominant ideologies of who a scholar is and what scholarship is valid, the authors herein challenge the rigidity of the academy by underscoring their deeply transformative paths to discovering their own kinds of scholarship. Using a critical lens, these scholars redefine and reshape intellectual thought. Centering their raced experiences, they shine a spotlight on the counter-narratives of doctoral students of color and the ways in which their existence is supported, validated, and nurtured. In this section, the scholars of colors share the struggles and successes in coming to know what it means to be a scholar, defining it for themselves and, therefore, developing a scholarly identity.

1   Who's the Scholar?

Emerald Templeton

I didn't see myself in a lab coat, or crunching numbers in the wee hours of a study session huddled around a computer screen. My vocabulary didn't save space for coefficients, multivariables, anovas, data—anything I perceived as research.

For as far back as I can remember, my educational experiences were littered with notions that (1) I was not as smart as others around me and (2) achieving academically would be by sheer luck. I remember struggling with math and science in school, and even, carrying deep guilt and anxiety about the difficulty in learning and using statistics at the graduate level. So, the first time I heard a faculty member refer to me as a scholar and researcher, you may be able to imagine the comic disbelief (and terror) that swirled around in my mind. Of course, I was enrolled in a doctoral program, and that required at least a moderate amount of academic ability. But, I could not see myself as a scholar or researcher—it sounded like too large of a bill to fit and too big of a bite to chew. My journey to recognizing and refining a scholarly identity required getting beyond myself and society's ideals regarding who fits the mold.

Contending with Society's Stereotypes

In Claude Steele's *Whistling Vivaldi*, he described Stereotype Threat as a standard human predicament in which we are threatened to be reduced to what others may think of us based upon generalized (and biased) social identities. Managing this predicament was not an unfamiliar task for me as it colored so many of my decisions from what I would wear to class, to how much I read and took notes, to how and when I would participate in class discussions. I think I spent more time worried that my colleagues and professors might think I wasn't prepared or that I didn't have the ability to perform up to or beyond the standard, than I did sitting with my thoughts about myself. Contending with the intersectionally marginalized identities of a Black woman, I was keenly aware of the deficit narratives that exist about my academic abilities, social status, and womanhood. The stereotypes of the "angry Black woman," "other mother," and the "lazy student" were looming over me as I tried to find the best way to show up as my authentic self. If a colleague said something racist or gendered in class and I reacted, I was unreasonably angry. If a White student started to cry when the topic of race was broached, I and other students of color were expected to care for them. When I kept my comments at bay, some of my colleagues assumed I wasn't prepared for class or that I didn't have anything meaningful to say. The fear of being relegated to these lesser, fictitious versions of myself caused me to be torn between who I am and who others expected me to be.

Feeling Like an Imposter

There's an old saying that "we are our own worst critics." When it came to pursuing an advanced degree, and traversing the academy in which few looked like me, I couldn't help but to feel like an imposter. I remember taking a course designed for supporting writing toward publication. Early on, I determined that I wanted to impact the field by writing about experiences like my own but was so doubtful that I had anything worth writing. Did I have a valid research topic? Would research on Black students be seen as scholarly work? So, I began writing about the development of diversity programs and whether they truly fulfilled their missions. I struggled with feeling pulled toward writing in a "neutral" territory. And, I thought, "Who am I?" as if I were intruding on writing about Black students or diversity—and writing as a researcher.

I was finding that the ways in which Black students were being written about in literature was often from a deficit lens. Despite the intentions of highlighting disparities in education, Black students were being discussed as if we were a problem needing to be fixed. Reflecting on my experiences and the messages I received throughout my life from media, teachers, and even some colleagues, higher education was depicted as unattainable, or difficult to attain, at best. When I discussed my academic and career goals, I was met with disbelief and disdain as if I wouldn't be able to achieve what I set out to, or that I didn't deserve the height of my pursuit. I felt like an imposter.

The System of White Supremacy and Education

As I began to progress in my learning and unlearning, it became apparent how pervasive and detrimental the system of whiteness is to education. My view of research, scholarship, and writing seemed so far from my identity because I was defining those items by the measure of whiteness. From the representations in literature to those individuals presenting at conferences, I had little positive view of myself in the scholarly space. When I was exposed to scholars of color, I often read and heard stories of their struggle for recognition and space. Some of the seminal works I read presented communities of color, Black communities specifically, from a deficit lens. And, those works were often written by non-Black scholars. To make matters worse, I heard of the difficulty in getting the work of Black scholars and other scholars of color published in top-tier journals and other prominent spaces.

Matching these sentiments, W. E. B. Du Bois, wrote about the "double-consciousness" of measuring myself against a White background. He described a "two-ness" that Black people in America must live with, often their competing identities as American and Black making the struggle of defining one's self a matter of deep, internal conflict. Much to Du Bois' point, I wanted my scholarship to be recognized and respected; rather than disappearing into the dominant, White framework for intellect, my work would emerge representing the truth of my scholarly identity centering blackness. And, holding onto the strength and resilience my blackness has given, I only hoped that I could navigate my scholarship as Du Bois described Black Americans navigating life: "without being cursed and spit upon by his fellows, without having the doors of Opportunity closed roughly in his face," (Du Bois, 2003, p. 9).

Scholarship as Justice and Intervention

Discovering my scholarly identity happened as a result of coming to understand my role in moving justice forward as interrupting the dominant narrative. So much of my doctoral experience involved socialization toward the academy, which defined scholarship and dictated who has the right to engage in scholarly work. Finding myself in this process required a shifting in my internal dialogue as well as an intervention in the conversations I navigated. With intention, I began talking with my colleagues about pushing our work into publication spheres. I began to see research as a tool for exploring solutions and writing as a venue for lifting the voices of the marginalized. I wanted the work of my Black colleagues to be recognized as scholarly and worthy of research, not only by others but ourselves.

Reference

Du Bois, W. E. B. (2003). *The Souls of Black Folk. (Barnes & Noble Classics).* New York, NY: Barnes & Noble (Original work published in 1903).

2 Doubt

The Uninvited Educator

Stephanie Aguilar-Smith

During the fall of my fourth year in my doctoral studies, I sat in my last graduate class—my program's capstone course in which students prepare their dissertation proposals. One by one, the professor asked us—this amalgam of eight or so students from different cohorts and with a range of unrelated research interests—to summarize our studies' problem statements, using a three-proposition approach:

- Proposition 1—State a fact or trend.
- Proposition 2—State a fact or trend that challenges Proposition 1.
- Proposition 3—Combine the propositions to illustrate the tension or problem at the core of the study.

One by one, my classmates, positioned in this makeshift circle of desks, presented their three-pronged problem statements. Following each, the professor, joined by the rest of the class, caringly critiqued each student's mastery of this formula. Had our peers actually identified a *researchable* problem?

As my turn neared, an unease crept into me, even though, at this point, my three-chaptered proposal was almost finished—a few minor edits from submission. Plus, my advisor, a no-nonsense Latina who mercilessly bled my pages with track changes, had read and reread it too many times since I first shared it with her some eight months prior. Nevertheless, reformulating my work into these three prescriptive propositions unnerved me, and it showed in my delivery. In three short sentences, I stumbled to cogently explain the problem undergirding my study on the equity of a federal grant program. And so, following my spiel, the professor politely issued some probing questions in which she gently challenged me about *if* and *how* to empirically research the equity of a policy. Equity, after all, is relative—a principle dependent on each person's values. With this concern, she encouraged me to explore trend data on the allocations to this program and to pursue the more direct question: "Who is benefitting and in what ways?"

Weary of disagreeing with this professor, whose experience spans my lifetime, I teetered but then said, "I know who receives these grants and how much they request. I'm not sure this data makes for a dissertation as much as it does a report." There I was again defending my research, which it seemed so many wanted to uncomplicate—to make smaller—although they used terms like "manageable," "feasible," and "doable." I didn't *doubt* the goodness of their intentions, but I also didn't question the merit of my study, even if, sometimes, I doubted myself.

In the following class, when I explained to the professor that I'd submitted my 155-page proposal and scheduled its defense, she met me, not with congratulatory remarks, but with questions. "Do you think you're ready? Do you want to stay in this class?" "What are your plans after graduation?"

In response to her last question, I offered my failsafe, go-to reply: "employment." As rehearsed hundreds of times before, I then added, "Ideally, I'd like a faculty position, but I know the market's competitive." As if studying me, she then said, "Well, as you prepare for the job market, you'll want to work on better *articulating* your research agenda."

With that, I strolled to my car inflated with pride. The next morning, during my customary phone call with my mom, I gleamed with the victory of finally finishing my proposal. However, as I shared with her the previous night's exchange, she paused, and her voice held a sternness not often marked in her cadence. "¿Ella te dudaba? ¿Porque te pregunto si estabas lista si ya tu advisor había aprobado tu proposal (She doubted you? Why'd she ask if you were ready if your advisor had already approved your proposal?)"

Hitting me with a series of questions—ones for which I did not have firm answers—I suddenly heard undertones in my professor's comments. The pride I'd felt slightly deflated, replaced with a mixture of anger entangled with self-doubt. I wondered if she asked those questions to all students in my position, or did she doubt *my* preparedness, specifically?

Long after ending that call, the word "articulate" cycled in my mind, and I cringed, knowing its very raced undertone (a point discussed at length in Alim and Smitherman's book, *Articulate While Black*). It replayed, as I remembered the many times I'd heard White people remark, with some hint of surprise, on the articulateness of a Black student, presenter—person. Shuffling through these memories—ones common in my upbringing in the suburban sprawl of Atlanta—I wondered if my White peers questioned their daily exchanges in this way. Perhaps, people did not speak of their articulateness, and maybe if they did, these words didn't infiltrate their self-confidence, but, at that moment, they did mine.

Again, academia had eroded a part of my confidence. By year four, however, I was intimately familiar with the many ways academia could distort your purpose, molding something once beautiful into something repulsive. That is, academia subtly, yet pronouncedly, seemed to shift or thwart the reasons I initially embarked on doctoral education. After all, I didn't pursue a PhD seeking to stand as some exemplar of the unsung ability of Latinx immigrants like me. That wasn't the point.

As a first-generation Venezuelan immigrant and a first-generation graduate student educated and employed at predominately White institutions, I began my PhD aware of how higher education disservices people and, especially, communities of color. As Brint and Karabel presented in their seminal text, *The Diverted Dream: Community Colleges and the Promise of Educational Opportunity in America*, I knew that a confluence of structural conditions *diverted* so many students, many from chronically underserved communities, from realizing their potential. I also saw the meritocratic idealization of higher education for the myth it so often is. And, I saw this system—one erected on stolen lands and built by forced labor—for what it is and what it does, defining some students as *deserving* and others as *disengaged*. Indeed, witnessing and experiencing such disservice, as both a student and a higher education professional, compelled me to pursue doctoral education. By gaining additional skills and knowledge, I hoped to work toward remedying some of the systemic issues pervasive throughout the US system of higher education. Invested in this purpose, I'd prepared for long days, endless readings, inane class assignments, and the compulsory bureaucratic hoops. However, I was unprepared for all I would come to know about higher education and, also, about myself.

Doctoral studies firmly educated me on just how suspicious academia is of change—even generative disruption. A los coñazos (through the blows), I learned that academia, particularly the field of higher education, is often still far too enamored with what has been than on the *radical possibilities* of what could be (hooks, 1994). With such myopia, inertia, and resistance define so much the academy. In a cruel sort of irony, the academy has normalized or institutionalized a suspicion, or perhaps cowardice, of what learning brings. That is, as I navigated my PhD, it clicked; the academy lives at odds with itself, holding up learning while wary of change.

Even with this understanding, I wasn't fully prepared for how to navigate this suspicious undercurrent—seemingly alone. As an immigrant, I was keenly familiar with the liminality and tensions Gloria Anzaldúa highlights as being *ni de aquí, ni de alla (neither from here, nor from there)*. Yet, within academia, I felt especially alone. In my program, I scarcely saw, read, or heard stories similar to mine, and I rarely met others who shared my commitment to the Latinx community. During my first year, I was one of only four Latinx PhD students in my department, which offers three doctoral programs, enrolling over 150 PhD and EdD students combined.

This loneliness deepened as the distance between my family and I grew both physically and otherwise. Although deeply proud of me, my family neither fully understood doctoral education nor the nature of my work. Paradoxically, the degree I pursued to live into my family's values—to live in service of nuestra comunidad (our community)—is also what estranged me from them. In what, at times, felt like an ugly zero-sum game, I gained schooling at the cost of much of their understanding.

In such a space, I ebbed in and out of doubt—not a paralyzing, all-consuming doubt. Instead, this doubt was one that stealthily resurfaced with each opportunity I earned. It reappeared when my peers questioned why I received an accolade, position, or grant. It was the perpetual, but an uninvited, guest. Although un coleado (a tagalong), doubt served as its own brand of education. Throughout doctoral education and all of academia's racism, sexism, nativism, linguism, and ableism—from all of its embedded horrors—I became convinced of at least a few of doubt's benefits.

Doubt imbued in me a steady skepticism; hell, it made me into a skeptic. As I cultivated doubt, I demanded more evidence. I read more scrupulously, heeding Levin-Morales's 1998 charge to carefully consider what was there and search for what was missing. I also listened more closely for peoples' often raced and gendered semantic moves and rhetoric, remembering both the work of Eduardo Bonilla-Silva and Nolan Cabrera. Meanwhile, doubt also made me confront the academy's deeply held investments—its allegiance to particular ways of researching, writing, and languaging, as well as its privileging of objectivity and apoliticism.

While searching in between the lines of texts, doubt also pushed me to find co-conspirators. It is because of doubt that during my PhD

I found brilliant scholars of color whose affirmations packaged away much of the self-doubt academia had gifted me, replacing it instead with belongingness. In so doing, over time, I slowly began to doubt my self-doubt, questioning instead those who microaggressed, infantilized, or *nicely* questioned the legitimacy of my ways of knowing.

Doubt, at least for me, was (and is) unavoidable in academia, but I've learned there is power in it too. Doubt cuts both ways. In doubting myself, I gained the strength to ask, what if I doubted them too? And, this move is a powerful form of resistance and a means of resilience.

Reference

Hooks, B. (1994). Teaching to transgress: Education as the practice of freedom. New York: Routledge.

3 The Last Dance
How I Learned to Stop Shuckin' and Jivin'

Angel M. Jones

I would love to say that being a PhD candidate at George Washington University is a dream come true, but that would be a lie. And that's not to say that what I'm doing isn't dream worthy, because it is. But, as a first-gen college student, becoming "Dr. Jones" was never on my radar. However, once the journey began, I was willing to do whatever it took to make my new dream come true, even if it meant losing myself along the way. This chapter describes that journey.

Acknowledging My Performance

In the spring of my second year, I wrote a poem about how silenced I felt as a Black woman at a historically White institution. I called it "Dance, girl" to represent the constant shuckin' and jivin'—a performative act—I had to do to survive.

Dance, girl
I am a performer
And not the type you see on stages, performing in front of millions of adoring fans
No, I'm the one that shucks and jives for my academic masters
You see, I'm a fully funded PhD student, which means the University pays for my tuition and living expenses
And as a first-generation college student, raised by a single mother in Brooklyn, I know that's a big deal
Started from the bottom now we here, right?
But "here" feels like a plantation
and I'm enslaved by the fear of one wrong move resulting in my academic lynching
So, when a white professor implies that me rocking my natural hair must mean that I am too stressed out to straighten out,

I curse her out.......
in my head
But what actually comes out sounds more like "ye'sa ma'sa"
Because I smile nervously and say....
nothing
I bite my tongue until it bleeds
And while the bright red blood stains my lips,
my silence paints my face black and I become their minstrel show
I make them smile, even though behind my own, I am crying
In the real world, I am proud Black woman, hear me roar
I blast salsa music in my car as the Puerto Rican flag on the rearview
mirror blows in the wind
I flip over tables of injustices, and I'm quick to check anyone who dares
to disrespect my people
But when I go to school, those parts of me stay home
With each step I take on campus, I shrink smaller and smaller
Until I've packaged myself in a way that is more palatable for white
people
I make them comfortable, and they love it
I am their house negro
I'm the one they introduce to company because they think I know my
place
But while my body is in the house, my mind is in the fields
And like Harriet, I am planning my escape
I perform publicly, but in private I am building my underground
railroad
So in the meantime, I'll keep dancing
Because I know that when the music stops,
They'll have to call me Doctor

Although writing the poem was therapeutic because it allowed me to speak my truth, I was simultaneously ashamed of it. I knew that I had a tendency to shuck and jive at school but realizing the extent of it stung in a way that I wasn't ready for. I felt like a fraud. I had dedicated my entire career to empowering students to be their authentic selves, but there I was shrinking myself to placate and pacify White people. I also felt unfit to call myself a critical race scholar, because how could I speak out against racial injustice when my silence often made me complicit in it? Yet, despite being utterly disgusted by my performance, I kept dancing.

I kept dancing because I was afraid of the consequences of stopping. If I called out my racist professor, would my grade suffer? What if I called out the racist institution—would my funding suffer? I wasn't prepared to find out, so I kept my mouth shut and kept on dancing. Unfortunately, I was so worried about protecting my academic standing that I forgot to protect myself. My grades may not have suffered, but my mental and physical health definitely did. I was struggling with a severe case of racial battle fatigue—the negative psychological and physiological consequences of consistent and prolonged exposure to racial microaggressions. But had no idea (which is ironic and embarrassing since it is something my research focuses on).

Psychological symptoms of racial battle fatigue include anxiety and depression, both of which I struggled with heavily. I remember a stretch of time that lasted for about a month when I cried every single day. I was absolutely miserable. I dreaded the idea of having to go to campus because I knew someone was going to do or say something racially disrespectful, and I would just have to take it (I know now that I didn't *have* to take it, but I hadn't learned that lesson yet). Although I experienced microaggressions from various White people on campus, there was one specific professor that was a repeat offender. Knowing that I would have to interact with him used to cause me so much anxiety that it would wake me up in the middle of the night. I started seeing a psychiatrist and was put on medication in the fall of 2018 because of my depressive symptoms. By the spring of 2019, my psychiatrist told me that he believed that the best course of action for me was to remove myself from the situation, which would have meant dropping out of the program. This was not an option that I was willing to consider, so I fought through the tears and kept on dancing.

While I had convinced myself that I could handle the psychological symptoms of racial battle fatigue, the physical symptoms were a different story. I already struggle with a heart condition that is typically managed by a pacemaker that is implanted in my chest. It is programmed to kick in whenever my heart rate drops suddenly. My anxiety had gotten so bad that my pacemaker would go off every time I received an email notification because I thought it might be from the professor I mentioned earlier. This eventually became too much for my heart to handle and landed me in the hospital, twice. The doctor informed me that my heart was not equipped to handle the amount of stress I was experiencing and recommended that I do whatever I could to minimize my stress.

Based on the advice I got from both my psychiatrist and my doctor, it was clear that something had to be done. While I hate that it took laying in a hospital bed for me to realize the importance of prioritizing my health over the placation of White people, I am glad I finally got the message. At that moment, I decided that I was going to stop allowing myself to be silenced by fear. If I should've been afraid of anything, it should've been what might have happened to me if I had kept dancing. Was I really going to shuck and jive until it killed me? Absolutely not.

Lessons Learned

In order to truly value and prioritize my well-being, I had to change the way I thought, which ultimately changed the way I moved. Although I have learned many lessons as a result of my experience, there are two that stand out the most. First, I learned how dope I am, which was, by far, the hardest lesson I had to learn (and definitely the most important). I believe most doc students struggle with Impostor Syndrome. I think that there is an added burden for people of color in predominantly White spaces because our competency is consistently called into question by our White students, peers, and faculty. However, when I feel myself starting to buy into their racist rhetoric, I have learned to combat those thoughts by reminding myself that I belong here. PERIOD. At the end of the day, I was admitted into this program because they saw my potential and believed that I was worth investing in. Yes, me, the first-generation, Afro-Latina from Brooklyn, is worthy. And not just because *they* think so, but because it's true. Relying on the opinions of others will not sustain me. I had to acknowledge my own dopeness and operate from a strengths-based mindset in order to endure and persist. Are there things that I don't know? Of course. Are there times I feel absolutely clueless in class? Yup. But, so what. I am a student. I'm here to learn and that's exactly what I am doing. So, instead of dwelling on the things I don't know, I've learned to focus on the things that I bring to the table. I walk into every room with knowledge and experiences that no one can touch or take away from me. Once I started seeing myself as a contributor, it totally changed my perspective on who and what I am. I am dope, and so are you.

Second, I learned that it is not just ok to be my authentic self, but it is crucial. As I mentioned earlier, "performing" was second nature to me and it started as soon as I stepped foot on campus. During my first semester, I really struggled with figuring out how to "be" in this space. I was constantly having silent conversations in my head about what was "appropriate"—"Is it appropriate to say that?" "Is it appropriate to do that?" "Is it appropriate to wear that?" It was exhausting, but it was what I did to survive. But after ending up in the hospital, I decided that being *me* was appropriate. This meant I no longer had to modify my resistance by wearing a blazer over my "We Out" shirt. This meant I could now allow my Latina accent to come out when I speak without turning beat red because it slipped. But most importantly, it meant I no longer had to bite my tongue when someone said something derogatory about Black and Brown people. Because I no longer allow my behavior to be dictated by the fear of what others may think of me, I am now able to bring my authentic self into all spaces, on and off campus.

Although I may have entered the hospital broken and defeated, I left it unapologetic—unapologetically Black, unapologetically Latina, unapologetically Brooklyn, and, most of all, unapologetically me. And I intend to leave this institution the exact same way.

4 Finding an Academic Voice in Place of Isolation

Christy Wynn Moland

I am what is referred to as an academic inbreed because I attended the same university for all three of my degrees. As an undergraduate in the Communication Sciences and Disorders Department, I was one of nine African American students in a class of 90. From the beginning, I had a circle of friends from whom I could draw strength and support. As a master's student, I was the only African American student in a class of 20–25. My peers were always welcoming, and I still had a circle of friends, but something about being the only one that looked like me made me feel isolated. When I started my doctoral program, I was anxious to discover what, if anything, would be different about this experience. In my PhD program research lab, there were six students. It was hard for me to believe but this time I was one of three African American students. The two other African American students and I started the program and took the same basic classes; however, we had divergent study paths. There were other African American students in the other research labs in our program and we all bonded on some level. However, the closest bonds were between people within the same lab. It was always as if others connected on a greater level with each other than with me. Although I started to build connections with other African American doctoral students both inside and outside of my department, it was against the backdrop of isolation that I pursued my doctoral studies.

There were many unwritten program expectations that I learned while matriculating. I needed to pass a general exam—containing both oral and written components—prior to starting my dissertation. While I always excelled in classes, I found myself silent for fear of being judged. Positioning myself solely as a listener in front of academic crowds, I was perceived as timid or shy. I remember presenting in my department and the sight of the familiar faces in the crowd overwhelmed me to the point of shutting down. My personal insecurities played out professionally, as a result, I did not travel to present at as many conferences as my peers at the beginning of my program. I wanted to be seen as an emerging scholar, but my feelings of isolation hindered me. For close to a year, I focused my attention on preparing the papers I needed for the exam. For my entire master's program, I trained to become a speech-language pathologist, it was ingrained in me to "think like a clinician." Now at the oral defense of my general exam, I quickly realized that I was expected to think like a scholar. This was a sobering thought that made for a hard transition.

Transitioning from clinician to scholar, I realized that I had to shift from being told what to do and how to do it but rather to have independent thought. I was given the space to grow and to execute. I began working on both individual and collaborative lab projects. In the past, I was assigned one project at a time, but now I was responsible for many tasks. My major professor, a mentor who served as my dissertation committee chair and academic advisor, was my primary support system within the department during my doctoral studies. Our relationship dates back to my undergraduate studies. I was a junior when she first introduced me to research and gave me the opportunity to do research under her tutelage. She guided my undergraduate thesis project and served as my master's thesis committee chair. I greatly valued this relationship because it endured and helped shape my academic identity. Although I regressed at the start of my doctoral journey, I had already traveled to and presented at conferences both in and out of state before I began working on my doctorate. The hours that she spent teaching me how to do research, design posters, and write up my findings long before I began the doctoral studies proved to be the foundation of my scholarly identity. She encouraged me to give guest lectures in classes inside and outside of my department in order to increase my comfort level in the classroom. I subsequently became a teacher's aide for two different courses. In one course I only graded assignments, while in the other I regularly taught. Teaching for an entire semester helped me become at ease in the classroom. I found my voice and began taking charge when meeting with other instructors in my discipline.

Doctoral students were required to present at our monthly departmental Brown Bag meetings, and my anxiety was the highest in this situation. I am not sure why I found it so difficult to present in front of all these people I knew—I would usually want to go in a corner and hide. However, as I progressed in my program, I felt better about getting in front of this group and sharing my research. I volunteered as a clinical supervisor for master's level students at local Head Start programs and coordinated the speech and hearing screenings at these facilities. During this time, I not only supervised the students, but I discussed procedures with the Head Start directors and classroom teachers.

There was something about being toward the end of my program that caused an internal shift. I began speaking out. I was often called upon to meet with students who were interested in studying in our lab. As new members joined the lab, I welcomed them and made it a point to make myself available to them. I shared information with those who were newer to the program. Just as some helped me along the way, I wanted to pass that help on to others. I told them what to expect in the program, and I shared my personal experiences, not to influence them, but to let them know that they could make it, just as I was making it. I wanted them to see that they could ask me anything, and I would be open and honest. At this point, I was also given the opportunity to mentor an undergraduate student preparing for graduate school. Not only was I sharing my knowledge and experiences with the new students, but I also started to own who I was as an academic. My confidence increased. I initiated activities and spoke up during lab meetings. I felt more comfortable presenting. I was no longer that shy, timid academic. I started to realize that I was just as deserving as others I encountered on my doctoral journey. I could see the light at the end of the tunnel. The end was in my view.

One of the biggest breakthroughs for me was at my prospectus presentation. This was my first meeting with my dissertation committee after the oral defense of my general exam. It was here that one of my committee members commented on watching my scholarly development. I remembered receiving remarks regarding my confidence that were diametrically opposed to the feedback I was given at my general exam. After my prospectus, one of my dissertation committee members invited me to meet with a group of female professors from the university who were having lunch with a visiting professor that was highly regarded in the academic community. This gave me the opportunity to socialize and interact with people on the same level as I would need to grant me access to do my research.

As I continued to develop my research identity, I was able to use the experience of my lunch meeting to develop inroads into the tight-knit research community. I had opportunities to give recruitment talks in the local community where I initiated meetings with individuals in both the school system and Head Start programs regarding my proposed work. My scholarly identity matured. I presented at conferences without the accompaniment of my major professor in tow. Throughout the dissertating process, she affirmed my knowledge, research, and progression toward completion. On the day I walked into my defense, I was not the timid, shy Christy. I walked in as a confident scholar. I remember making jokes with my committee members and laughing and talking with colleagues and friends who waited to watch me defend. I trained for the last six years and the time had finally come. I commanded the room. I presented, answered questions, smiled, and exuded all the confidence of a scholar. I knew I was different, and I knew I was meant to be at that lectern at that moment.

My journey to becoming an academic scholar was filled with a lot of opportunities for me to mature and flourish both personally and academically. I went from being an insecure, reticent graduate student to an accomplished researcher. I navigated through situations at the end of my program with ease that would have crippled me in the beginning. I emerged confident with advanced skills and a renewed sense of self. My maturation as a scholar was recognized and respected by others. One of the biggest contributors to my success was a major professor that supported me as a person and regarded me as a professional. Was it easy? NO. Did it take years to prepare? YES. Was it worth it? Absolutely!

Since completing my doctorate degree, I have served on professional committees within my field, mentored graduate students through capstone projects, served as both an assistant clinical director and clinical director of a University Speech and Hearing Clinic, supervised graduate students in clinical settings, and been an assistant professor. Today, I maintain connections with students who still reach out to me years after they graduated. This warms my heart because I am able to pay forward what I received and what was modeled for me. I continue to maintain a relationship with my major professor. In recent years, we have co-presented in the community and at national conferences and worked on publications together. When I began my doctoral program, I did not know how it would all turn out. My road to scholarship was enhanced by the presence of my major professor who believed in me from the very beginning. I am a respected practitioner in speech-language pathology and the woman who was once my major professor is now my professional colleague. We teach at the same University with offices side by side.

5 "They Called Diversity a Nuisance Variable"

Ivan Carbajal

An Identity in Crisis

A few years ago, my psychology department hosted a symposium on diversity in research. The only Latina faculty member and a White male faculty member, who is known for his work in cultural humility, hosted this symposium. Many of us at the symposium *tried* to discuss what diversity meant in terms of research, but what ended up occurring transformed our department, for better or worse. Here is a quick highlight of the main points our faculty discussed at the symposium: diversity research will not advance your career, testing your theory on different groups of people is a waste of time, all theories generalize to all people, cross-cultural research is bogus because we all have the same brain structures, diversity should be likened to astrology, and—*perhaps my favorite*—diversity variables (i.e., demographics) are a nuisance. The Latina faculty had the impossible task of defending not only herself and her work, but also protecting the students of color that were stunned at hearing that their own faculty do not believe diversity is important. All of this was happening while the White male faculty, who again, is an expert in cultural humility, sat there in silence.

As graduate students, we were at a disadvantage. Power differentials made it so that even as we spoke against these beliefs, we were still just "lowly" students supervised by these faculty. We were mocked for our beliefs with comments that suggested we study "shrimpers" and "ballerinas" if we saw studying group differences as useful. We were told theoretical work on ethnic, sexual, and gender minorities was hard to find, while examples of the minority stress model, cultural differences in attachment styles, and racial trauma were ignored.

It was at this moment when I learned that my being, my existence as a brown Latino, mattered more than anyone ever led me to believe.

At times, I feel so naïve when I reflect on my past in my graduate program, where I felt I owed my first advisor for being in graduate school. Putting up with plenty of microaggressions because I thought to myself, "hey, just be glad you are here." As graduate students, we all face Imposter Syndrome; we hardly feel like we belong or are smart enough to be where we are. However, as *graduate students of color* we also have to battle thoughts of tokenism, where we think that we are only here because we check the box for diversity. There is this inter-sectional doubt we experience where not only do we feel like we don't belong, but we see ourselves as less than everyone else because of the color of our skin, our gender, our sexual orientation, etc. It was because of this doubt that I let myself be humiliated at times by faculty. The events that unfolded after this symposium initiated a lot of change within me.

Navigating Identities

I experienced an awakening in my own identity. I am a first-generation Mexican American and college student. Moving to the town where I lived for graduate school was the first major life decision I ever made on my own. It was the first time in my life that I was no longer bound by family obligations and cultural expectations. I felt like I was finally free to be myself. However, my first year in graduate school was tough. I no longer had my support group. I was in a town where there was not a vibrant Mexican community. To top things off, I was a part of a cohort of 15 where only two of us were students of color; the rest were all White. I was in a place where, culturally, no one understood me, and I had no community with whom I could voice my woes. There was this great need to fit in, so I learned and did what I had to do to fit in with my White peers. There is nothing worse than hearing "you're so Mexican" when surrounded by people you would be colleagues with for the next five years. So you readjust yourself, you lose your cultural identity, you do not bring things up that you think are "too Mexican," and most of all, you do not focus your career on studying Mexicans and Latinxs.

All of these feelings went away when I heard my then advisor say that a focus on diversity in research would not land me a career. I felt as if my being did not mean anything. That my *Latinidad* was being attacked. That I worked for an advisor that did not believe my experiences as a graduate student of color were real. This was a catalyst in not only reawakening my identity as a Latino but as a Latino researcher. For three years, I worked for someone that made me believe studying group differences was not important, so I internalized the beliefs that I had to be just a researcher, and that being Latino did not matter. I did a lot of self-reflection on what it meant to be a Latino in graduate school. No one else in my entire department (of around 75 graduate students) was Latinx, so there was never anyone I could talk to about my experiences, until our Latina faculty came in. Talking to her about my experiences was so cathartic. It was through her that I saw myself. I saw the way she seamlessly interwove her identity into her teaching and research. Her example taught me just how wrong our White male faculty were. I *can* make a career out of being myself. This was the beginning of embracing my Latinidad and my path toward social justice advocacy and cultural research. Perhaps the proudest, and the most profound, thing that came out of the conversations with the Latina faculty was that she allowed me to reclaim my name with the accent and all.

After the fallout of the symposium, our department went into panic mode. Emails were sent around that only assuaged the faculty's white fragility. It became very clear to the students that our faculty would never take the students seriously when it came to our grievances. So, we did what any good researcher would do—collect data. Alongside my best friend, the other student of color from my all White cohort, we created a survey that asked about the climate in our department and how inclusive it was to various minoritized groups. For a department that touted that they did "diversity well" the results of our survey were shocking for our White faculty and validating for our students of color. Across the board, we found that our department did not, in fact, do diversity well.

Finding Myself

Quantifying our pain was the only way our faculty and department finally realized they needed to act. Our university's Office of Equity and Diversity was called in to train faculty, staff, and students about creating more inclusive spaces. I wish I could say that after their intervention that everything in our department was magically healed, but I cannot. There are now those faculty who are on their path to becoming allies, some even accomplices (in social justice terms). However, a good portion of the faculty considered the training to be a waste of time and full of weakly validated methods and research. Even after all the effort to make our voices heard and create a cultural shift in our department, it was hard realizing that not everyone's mind would be changed. There are some faculty who will never budge on their dated, racist ideas. Personally, this was and is still hard for me because I always dreamed of becoming a professor. However, I have already lost and found myself once in academia. I cannot bear to lose myself again.

Finding myself was all thanks to my peers, my fellow students of color. I always tell incoming students to find their community—someone or some group that will help them pull through this journey. I especially tell the new graduate students of color to make close bonds with other people of color. They will be the wood to knock on when others make them feel delusional and out of place. They are the ones that will understand what their White peers might not fully grasp. I advocate for our own safe spaces, and some of the best and meaningful moments in my graduate career have been what we call "PoC Nights," where we gathered and just talked about our experiences—at times there were tears, there was anger, there was laughter, and sometimes dancing when we needed it. Most importantly, there was a lot of understanding.

I reflect on my journey very often. There are times when I can't believe that I put myself through this, there are other times when I feel like this is what happiness feels like. Regardless, something I always come out with is thinking about who I am now—and I can't help but feel so proud. I wish first-year me could see who I am now, to instill some hope that "you *will* survive this" and that ultimately "*they* are lucky to have you here." I have suffered but I have also accomplished a lot in my graduate training. I helped found a social justice organization, created a peer mentorship program, advocated for accountability in student-faculty mentorship, and I continue to host PoC Nights. My research has flourished, and I finally feel like I found where I belong. Even though I will occupy spaces in the future wherein people will question my worth, where people will call me a "troublemaker," where my colleagues will believe diversity is a nuisance and hold racist beliefs; I know I will be okay. Because I am Mexican, I am a researcher, I am a social justice advocate, and I belong.

With that, I leave you, future doctor, with one final lesson: don't readjust yourself to fit in, don't lose your cultural identity, don't worry about being "too Mexican," and always feel free to focus your career on the study of your people.

6 Finding My Voice, Encouraging Myself, and Calling Out Gendered Racism

A Black Feminist Graduate Student's Note on How to Thrive Within the Academy

La Toya Council

In July 2017, I almost quit my PhD program. I was in my car, on my way to my summer job. At the time, I had just passed my qualifying exams and was preparing to enter my fourth year of doctoral studies. I began thinking about how proud my late mother would have been of me. I could hear her voice expressing joy in my educational achievements. And then I began to cry because I felt like a fraud. I felt that I hadn't achieved anything worthy of my mother's pride. Because my department and discipline constantly made me feel worthless and told me that I did not belong, I internalized the idea that I was not good enough. And so, in that moment, I held my head down because I was too tired to continue. But I did not give up. Instead, I forged ahead—despite the relentless messages, both subtle and overt, from faculty and others in academia, that I am not supposed to be a member of the Ivory Tower. And I learned critical lessons along the way that I will share here.

I didn't always feel the way I felt in that moment. When I first entered my program, I was excited to start my PhD journey. I knew there would be challenges, but I was not prepared for the extent of the systemic racist and sexist encounters I experienced in my first four years. During the second semester of my first year, I experienced gendered racism for the first time in my life. In the middle of my presentation on Black social thinker, Frantz Fanon, my theory professor mapped the "Angry Black Woman" stereotype on my body. He interrupted my presentation by arguing against my use of the concept "Whiteness"— even though I was quoting directly from Fanon. He proceeded to take over my presentation, explaining how Fanon conceptualized race in *Black Skin, White Masks*. I felt myself going inward, trying to hold back tears that were shining at the brim of my eyes. When I was no longer able to hold my tears back, I excused myself and went to the restroom to cry. Doubts bubbled up: What did my new cohort mates think of me? Am I in over my head by attempting to do PhD-level work? After ten minutes, I went back to class. Before dismissing us, the professor turned to me and asked, "LaToya, are you still angry?" At this point, my embarrassment had reached new levels, and my only response was, "I'm not angry, just disappointed." Whether he realized it or not, his mapping of the "Angry Black Woman" stereotype on my body reverberated for the remainder of the semester with my mostly White colleagues. I noticed the cautious expression on their faces each time I spoke up and out in class. That single experience created a context for my classroom interactions in which it became hard for me to shine academically.

Given this unsupportive context, it was unsurprising that my performance was lackluster in that first year. Like many early-career graduate students, I was trying to find my ground. I entered my second year determined to excel by making all A's. It mattered to me because I knew that I was behind. I spent nights reading class material countless times and looking up words and scholars to make sure that I was prepared for each class. Midway through the semester, I received my performance letter. Despite my efforts, faculty described my underperformance as a concern that I would not do well in graduate school. Some even suggested that although I had great ideas, my inability to commit to a project proved that I may not belong in graduate school. The director of graduate studies at the time told me that some faculty wanted me dismissed from the program. I left her office feeling defeated. After multiple conversations with friends, I decided to continue pushing forward in my academic pursuits. This included meeting with professors during office hours to ensure I was making good progress. When I turned in my final paper for one course, I was happy because I had turned it in on time and put in a lot of hard work. I was surprised over winter break when I received a B in the course. I emailed the professor and was taken aback by a laundry list of all the things that were wrong with my paper. I was confused because I had met with the professor during office hours about this same paper. They had not mentioned any of these issues, all of which I could have easily fixed with timely feedback. I felt defeated due to my department's failure to provide mentorship and support toward my academic endeavors.

Three things occurred during my third year that changed my perception of academia and my feeling of belonging. These experiences also caused my stress levels to reach a height I had never experienced. First, the number of Black students in my program dropped from five to three (that following spring 2018, our program dismissed yet another Black student, leaving only myself and another woman by fall 2018). Second, I had worked hard on my qualifying exams, to the point that one professor raved about how "shocked" he was about my strong performance. Third, I was asked to take on mentor responsibilities for a fellow Black colleague who suffered from mental health issues combined with departmental racism.

Spring 2018, I was asked to take on *unpaid* peer-mentoring work. In addition, I was dealing with being one of only a handful of Black graduate students remaining, dealing with a professor who outwardly expressed his disbelief in my ability to do graduate-level work. These experiences compounded graduate school's tolls on my personal and mental health. I started binge eating more. I even felt guilty for going to bed at night—waking up in sweats trying to catch my breath. I felt behind, even though I was moving at the same pace as my peers. This state of high stress started during my qualifying exams but persisted afterward. I remember days sitting at my computer with shaking hands, attempting to write a manuscript for peer review. I was unable to put words on paper. My mind was fuzzy, and I was in a perpetual state of inarticulation. I could only focus on being one of three Black students remaining in my program, and I wondered when I would receive a letter stating that I was no longer a great fit for our program. I was scared, knowing that if I was dismissed, I would be walking into the arms of poverty. All these accumulated experiences of institutional racism and sexism led my blood sugar, blood pressure, and weight to increasingly spiral out of control. The devastation on my health was so serious that my doctor asked me "if I planned to die early." I was on a dangerous path, unaware, and with no direction on how to turn it around.

That moment made me realize that I needed to turn things around if I wanted to survive. I successfully applied for and won fellowships to remove myself from my department and move to Washington, DC to conduct fieldwork in my fifth year. As a result, I healed, recharged, and reconnected with why I decided to enter academia. Because of this, I am in a much healthier space mentally, physically, emotionally, and spiritually. From these experiences, I have learned that there are four things that I should keep in mind when navigating the trauma academia so often heaps on students of color.

First, it is imperative to prioritize mental, physical, emotional, and spiritual well-being. When I moved to DC, I did so by throwing myself into self-care. I dedicated myself to happiness, joy, and personal self-definition because I realized that if I do not radically care for me, then no one else will. I took the rage I had boiling within, critically engaged key Black feminist texts, and set out on a personal journey to become a Black feminist who defines myself for myself. I went back to Patricia Hill Collins's *Black Feminist Thought*, Audre Lorde's famous essay on radically caring for self, bell hook's *All About Love*, and Brittney Cooper's *Eloquent Rage: A Black Feminist Discovers Her Superpower*. By caring for my mental, physical, emotional, and spiritual health, I poured love into me. Caring for myself means creating boundaries around my time and academic commitments: my research is just one important element of who I am.

Second, I decided to seriously choose committee members that were committed to my development. I realized that while important names are nice, it should not be at my personal expense. It was important for me to find faculty in my program who would serve as sounding boards and listening ears, and I placed them on my committee. It is critical to have a committee that is invested in my development as a scholar. It is critical to have at least one person on my committee that I could trust and be "real" with. I have been able to create a committee that I call "my team." I know that each member of my dissertation committee is invested in my personal well-being and my academic career. I brag that I am blessed because of their commitment.

Third, I had to create a network of scholars who have become mentors and friends that includes graduate students in my department and graduate students at other universities, and faculty from different departments on my campus, as well as from other universities. Those students and faculty are my virtual writing supporters, feedback givers, and sounding boards when I need advice on personal matters that may impact my academic work. I don't take these friendships for granted, and I make sure I pour into them as much as they pour into me. A creative social justice children's book I co-authored came out of this network. *Intersection Allies: We Make Room for All* represents a pivotal moment when my personal healing meshed with my empowerment as a scholar and public intellectual. Writing our book allowed me to stay committed to community, stay committed to social justice, and draw on my and my colleague's academic wisdom as women of color.

Fourth, I have learned to become open to faculty who are *willing* to rewrite past harms. Some people may be more aware of their actions than others. For this, I live by my mother's advice. She taught me that it is pitiful to go through life and not extend grace to others. When professors and colleagues who have harmed me placed a foot forward to rewrite their past harms, I decided to make room for them. We did not become friends, but I learned to lean into how they were trying to move through and accept the harms they committed against me. When I was in the program, I had an opportunity to share my experiences as a Black woman in our department at our Town Hall. Afterward, the faculty emailed me to apologize for the treatment I experienced in the classroom, and their contribution in my feeling like I did not belong in academia. Receiving an outpour of apology, helped me move forward, and continue toward achieving my academic goals. Because of my willingness to extend grace, I have been able to work toward healing.

Enacting these strategies helped me begin to heal. They have also helped me stay committed to my passion in conducting research, producing knowledge, engaging activism, and staying committed to community. It is unfortunate that in 2020, we are still concerned with institutional racism, sexism, homophobia, and transphobia. I may not have the power to change the institution, nor should I be tasked to. But I can use my voice to speak out when I need to, and most importantly, speak within and encourage myself.

7 I Am Exactly Where I Need To Be...

Kayon A. Hall

I never imagined myself as a researcher or working in education. In fact, I dreamed of becoming a buyer because I was obsessed with fashion and home décor. However, growing up with a mother who is an educator, the seed to advocate for those most vulnerable was planted early. And what I have come to learn in life is, sometimes you end up doing the things you were meant to do, and you end up exactly where you need to be, even if that was not your plan.

Movement

I am a foreign-born Black woman from Jamaica who moved to the United States as a teenager when I learned about the US, particularly as related to the color of my skin. I was moving from a country where the organizing factor was social class to a country where race was the salient identity marker. Oftentimes I found myself silent in conversations about racial inequities because I thought I had no experience with racism or white supremacy, even though I was familiar with and had experienced colorism. How I formed and understood my racial identity as a Black woman was shaped by my former environment, and at the time, I did not have the tools to make sense of my experiences. I was not aware of how I would be racialized as a Black person in the United States or how Black people and other people of color are impacted by larger systems such as immigration and white supremacy.

As I got older and the more I read and learned through my own experiences, I began to understand the interconnectedness of race and larger oppressive structures. I began to realize that despite my ethnic background, my race was the most salient identity marker, and with that came challenges. As I continued to educate myself, I came across the work of Roy Bryce-Laporte, a West Indian sociologist from Panama. Bryce-Laporte wrote extensively about Black immigrants and what happens when foreign-born Blacks move from their pre-dominantly Black countries to the United States, where Black people are marginalized. Bryce-Laporte said foreign-born Blacks faced "double invisibility," that of being Black and that of being a foreign-born Black individual. His work set me on a path to examine and understand the experiences of foreign-born Black individuals and, essentially, myself.

The Field

My entry into higher education/student affairs was not an intentional move because I did not know such a field existed. However, just as how I fell into the field, I also fell in love with it. In my first job in higher education, I worked primarily with Black and Brown students because of the location of the school and the community we served. Working with these students, I began to develop deep relationships with them because we shared many of the same experiences. Like me, many of them moved to the United States and were processing what it meant to be Black, and what it meant to be placed in a racial category coming from a country where a pan-ethnic identity was how they identified. As I continued to gain more experience in higher education and work with students, I realized that I needed to do more. I needed to completely immerse myself in a space that would allow me to focus on learning as much as I could about myself and the students with whom I worked.

Representation in Research/Forming a Scholarly Identity

By the time I started applying for PhD programs, my research interest was set. I wanted to understand the experiences of foreign-born Black students.... I wanted to do me-search. Me-research is research that involves some aspects of one's identity or personhood. And for me, I wanted to learn more about people who looked like me and who had a transnational background. My journey to understanding my racial and transnational identity influenced the development of my scholarly identity.

I started my graduate program and was excited about the courses, my research interest, and the community of support I was building. But, as I navigated the graduate space, I found myself, more often than not, in conversations that centered students with marginalized identities. While I was happy to have these conversations, I quickly realized that the conversations were flat, or in other words, they lacked a nuanced racialized analysis. Discussions about Black students, specifically, focused on US-born Black students and their experiences but not foreign-born Black students. I was surprised because I am a foreign-born Black woman, and I grew up with several Black people who were also born outside the United States and who moved at various stages in their lives. I realized that although there are scholars who talk about the ethnic diversity among Black students (see Chrystal George Mwangi, Mary C. Waters, Barbara Thelamour's work), "Black students" did not mean or include foreign-born Blacks.

As conversations ramped up about undocumented students across college campuses and in society in general, I noticed, again, that Black people were left out of the "undocumented" conversation. I would go to conferences and attend presentations that highlighted the educational experiences of undocumented students, but I never heard about the experiences of Black students who are also undocumented. I would leave these conferences feeling low because the educational experiences of undocumented Black students were left out of the discourse. While I have never had an undocumented status, I grew up with, went to school with, laughed with, and broke bread with undocumented (those without citizenship or permanent residency in the United States) and DACAmented (those with temporary status under the Deferred Action for Childhood Arrivals legislation) Black folx. So why were their stories not being told? It was as if undocumented Black students were not impacted by policies and laws as they navigated the US educational system and the broader society. I started to think about Bryce-Laporte and how relevant his article written in 1972 was today and the double invisibility foreign-born Black folx face.

I decided that I would start bringing important insights to the undocumented conversation through my scholarship. I challenged my colleagues to think about Black people through an intersectional lens. Not just the relationship between race and white supremacy, patriarchy, or capitalism, but also through citizenship. I critiqued theoretical frameworks I learned in class that were often used to examine the Black experience because they were shortsighted in accounting for other overlapping identities such as citizenship status. I sought out opportunities that would allow me to teach and talk about undocumented/DACAmented Black students. I learned from and alongside undocumented/DACAmented Black students to shift, complicate, and build upon the field of higher education's understanding of undocumented/DACAmented students. I questioned because the paradox of education, as James Baldwin notes, is such that, as I became conscious, I started to examine the society in which I was being educated.

A Call to the Field of Higher Education

I realized that the work that I was doing was important, not because there was a "gap" in the literature, but because of the *double invisibility* and the in-betweenness Ijeoma Umebinyuo pointed to in her poem. Ijeoma's poem, Diaspora Blues, powerfully highlights the tension between never being enough for any particular place and being caught in the middle. This in-betweenness Ijeoma speaks of impacts me as a foreign-born Black woman navigating a society that requires me to fight for visibility and informs how and why I engage in research that centers undocumented Black students. Undocumented/DACAmented Black students are caught in the intersections because they are not seen or imagined as being undocumented. I am especially reminded of this invisibility whenever I discuss my research, and I see furrowed brows that are immediately followed by the "undocumented Black students?" question.

Cultural theorist, Stuart Hall, or Uncle Hall as I so affectionately call him, talked about the importance of mobilizing intellectual resources to understand why the world we live in is so profoundly inhumane. I continuously ask myself, what are the different ways I can use my intellectual resources to work with and alongside undocumented/DACAmented Black students and do so with love? So, I offer up the same message to the field of higher education to mobilize resources to identify the spaces that cause harm to all undocumented/DACAmented students.

Outro

I want to leave you all with a little golden nugget. Sometimes as we try to figure out our place in the world and in academia, we must quiet ourselves and leave our bodies in order to identify the signposts in our lives. My racial identity and my transnational background significantly influenced the development of my scholarly identity. And, as I worked to understand who I was/am as a Black woman in the US context, I was sowing the seeds for the scholar I am today. Lean into your own experiences and do not be afraid to let parts of who you are shape the scholar you become. So, you see, I am exactly where I need to be, and so can you.

With love,

Kayon

8   A 29-Year Journey Back to Radical Scholarship

Mignon Page-Broughton

I never gave much thought about my evolutionary journey to becoming a scholar. Recently, I finally questioned why I continued to stay involved with what, at times, I perceived as an emotionally abusive environment—academia. Personally, it has been a life-altering seven years, and a complex 29-year college journey. I was the first to go to college in my family. And yes, I said I've been in college for 29 years. Usually when you have conversations about writing your dissertation no one ever asks, "So how long have you been in pursuit of your collegiate studies?" Twenty-nine years. And, along the way, I've come upon several epiphanies.

Placing My Safety Net Aside

My expectations of my doctoral experience weren't congruent with my reality. Yet, I'm so grateful for the experiences. Three key themes illuminate for me. My doctoral experience was riddled with institutional hypocrisy, and experiences that pushed me to do and be better. I learned to understand my own identity as a cisgender woman of color while continuing to love and respect my foundation. Of equal importance, I had to embrace what completion represented for me. Twenty-nine years of triumphs and discomfort have formed my scholarly identity. As you read my thoughts, I hope you reflect on your own amazing narrative. And, that you show my vulnerable thoughts some grace.

A Member of the Collective But Now It's Time to Find My Way

My foundation was built on chaos, love, and acceptance of all humans. It consists of a lifetime of experiences, organic scholars also known as specialists/intellectuals who live in the community, folks who were not influenced by or formally trained within the academy. Yet, they engaged in academic discourse, and planted mustard seeds of knowledge that flourished during my studies. Radical scholars or non-conforming scholars who exist on the margins that I met along the way. My familial scholars from another mother that I connected with in my doctoral programs, my work scholars of color, and my mentor-professors from community college to my doctoral path studies. One particular mentor-professor lived in my neighborhood when I was a child. In my youth, he'd let me borrow books one at a time, and when I brought them back, we'd have discussions. As an adult, he helped me process my first sting to my scholarly psyche. And when I was accepted into my doctoral program that same mentor-professor explained that it was time for me to find my own way. To figure out what scholarship looked like to me. My base of guidance is imperishable. Yet, as I entered my doctoral program, I began to understand that my journey would be personal even though I was part of a collective community. While I came from a collectivist community, I now had to define myself as an individual while staying connected to my community. Throughout my studies, I examined my own history. Where I came from, who I was prior to my pursuit of a doctorate degree, and how the pursuit of a doctorate degree helped me expand my identity as a scholar.

My mother and grandmother were the center of my world. Both were single mothers always working two jobs while raising their children and fostering a love for education. To them, scholarship was gaining whatever knowledge possible and passing that knowledge onto the next generation. Grandmother was my first glimpse of a radical social justice scholar, a "we should all be feminist and love one another" scholar. My mother was also a "we aren't free until everybody's free" scholar. I always knew the community's definition, but I was never clear about my own definition of scholarship. I felt part of my doctoral journey had to be about me defining my own scholarship separate from the collective.

The Belly of the Academic Beast

I was oblivious to the politics of the academy. I had a few glimpses of bias, and ignorance during my prior studies, but nothing prepared me for my program. I was accepted into a program designed for working adults that had a social justice focus and catered to the research practitioner. My experience proved to be really eye-opening. I saw first-hand how marginalization and oppression played out in the education system. My program was cohort designed, and the first day of orientation the professors and students gathered and agreed I was an "other." I was already the only Black woman in the cohort when a tenured professor stated, "Since you don't work in the field of education, let's call you an 'other'." My first day, and I was strategically placed on the academic margin. At the afternoon session I met the only three professors of color. I sarcastically introduced myself as the newly appointed "other." One of the professors asked me to explain this title. She glanced toward the other two professors of color, then they proceeded to speak with the tenured professor who gave me the demeaning title. The tenured professor came to me and apologized by saying, "You're not the only 'other' [there's another student] who doesn't work in the educational field," as if this justified her comments. Although the professors of color spoke to the tenured professor—the tenured professor was unable or unwilling to understand how alienating her comment was.

Throughout the program, I noticed the tension in the space regarding the historically dominant voice, and how many times it was uncomfortable for those who weren't existing on the margins to share the academic space. I used to mark on the side of my notebook how many times students who did not identify as students of color interrupted those of us who are students of color. When interruption occurred, it was common practice to police the language and erudition of students of color. I also noticed how expectations were fluid depending on the student. If the criteria for an assignment had a page limit and a rubric, I was told all students had to meet the criteria or receive an automatic fail. Yet, I'd listen to White students share that they turned in a few pages and received an A. It was as if some students were part of a sub-program where rubrics and criteria did not matter. As the program moved forward, I noticed the White students and one Asian student began to question the students of color about their choice in research topics and committee member selection. During a class, each student announced their dissertation committee chair. I remember students questioning my, and my other Black colleagues', choice of a Black chair, noting that Black students just want Black committee members. Then the next student made a comment about my choice and another. Once we entered the classroom, I made it clear that no one should bring up race to me when speaking about my chair selection. I had the right to pick a chair that looked like me, but my selection was based on the fact that I had similar research interests to my chair. Each time someone crossed the line it always amazed me. The deeper we dove into the program and the research, the more students of color had to remind the cohort that we were in a social justice program. Every class I had to mentally prepare myself for some form of microaggression or inappropriate comment. I tried to stay focused on the process, the tools I was acquiring, and the reciprocity of ideas between those who were genuine within the space.

Walking My Own Path: Finding Peace

I also met an array of professors—some excellent, bad, and just plain ignorant. Each interaction shaped who I am today. One interaction that stands out in my mind was with the first professor I had who looked like me. I was at the end of my educational journey, and I was finally going to spend the semester with a Black female professor. I was so excited to meet her. She looked me up and down and did not shake my hand when I extended it before class started. Our first assignment was due in two weeks and I poured into it—or so I thought. It was a personal piece on what type of educator you think you are. The class was co-taught and both professors made it clear that the paper had to be clear, pithy, and three pages. During a break, the Black professor walked up to me, told me she read my paper, and I should quit. She said I did not have what it takes to be a scholar and that I was naïve to think that there was a place for me in the academy. What she did not know was the professor who was co-teaching with her was behind her when she spilled her vitriol onto me. She walked past me, and tears welled up in my eyes. The kind professor who overheard the exchange said, "Not only do you belong here, your powerful words brought me to tears." He went on to say, "If I had a dollar for every professor who thought my queer presence didn't belong in the academy, I'd be rich." On that day, the kind professor, who identified as a queer White male, took over the rest of the class to talk about educational privilege within communities of color and how colonized brainwashing continues to turn some people of color against others who look like them. As I think back, I just remember feeling deeply disappointed. No one prepared me for disappointment. Or what I'd have to give up in the quest for completing my doctoral studies.

I honor my communal foundation. It has influenced my journey, but I had to develop my own identity. Within the academy, I always felt repressed. At the beginning of the program, I observed really quick that parts of me were not palatable. It was like there was an unspoken expectation of me to change or shed my sense of self. My existence within the space could always be better—I had to always improve.

With each class, I grew determined that I had ownership within the space. I received the training and was open to the additional skills, but my journey became personal—it belonged to me. I fully engaged in every aspect of my doctoral studies, stayed open to each professor and student perspective, and analytical rationale. Close to two-thirds into the program I knew I did not want to mimic Eurocentric scholarship. My lens was one of resistance. My scholarship represented disruption to the system. Being *me* meant I approached research with authenticity, vulnerability, and emotion. Now, the same way I moved outside the ivory tower is the way I moved within it. Radical love, loving, and seeing myself and others through an equitable lens was my scholarly conceptual framework. My journey has been shaped by obstacles and hardships. I was ready to seek out my own joy in the latter part of the program in the form of reading works produced by scholars of color. I went to conferences that I wanted to attend, read articles that fed my soul. My journey was shaped by adversity, but equanimity became the center of my essence. A calmness started washing over me when folks in my program started talking foolishly during classes, or when professors who were not equipped to diffuse difficult conversations stayed quiet. I had begun to have grace for myself and others, grateful to be fully present in the academy as hegemony played out in real time.

My therapist asked me recently, "Why do you think you haven't finished your dissertation?" I joked that maybe I'm not ready to leave the abusive relationship called academe. For 29 years, I've had peers and professors question my existence within the space. I've been in a honeymoon-abuse cycle my whole adult life with the academy. Life has passed by. I've raised three children with the assistance of extended family. My grandson was born. My best friend died of cancer, family members died, my father and grandmother died. I've battled exhaustion, frustration, procrastination, and depression. For 29 years, I've chased the academic rainbow. I believe I haven't finished partially because of fear, but mostly due to my inability to define what completion looks like for me. My scholarship has been based on a strong foundation that was built outside the academy—now for me scholarship is an intersection of my identity outside the academy, my academic experiences, and my life interactions with global community members. My scholarship is defined by the reciprocity of knowledge exchanged, and the humbled privilege of working alongside members of the community in the pursuit of solidarity work. Scholarship is acquiring knowledge and being mindful of each person's journey. My foundational base is part of me, but it is not all of me. As I navigated my studies, I learned along the way that I was being chipped away. I thought I had to lose pieces of myself to be accepted. Yet, I have never quite been accepted. I've been a guest in my academic home for 29 years. My scholarship no longer conforms to the Eurocentric patriarchal ideology that the academy was built on. My scholarship is influenced by a global community. For me, completion is defined as my personal decision and if I chose, it can be fluid. Today, *completion* is that I have finished my coursework. No more no less. If tomorrow I decide completion looks different, then it will.

9 A Cautionary Tale

Linda Garrett

As I contemplated what information to share with you to make your journey easier, I thought about giving advice on choosing a topic, or your committee, or other practical words of wisdom that would make me sound super intelligent (after all, I am a "Whole Entire Doctor" out here in these streets). I recounted the words of Carter G. Woodson who raised the question about what it means to be educated. I sat staring at the computer screen, the blank page mocking me because none of the words in my vocabulary would arrange themselves into a coherent paragraph—I realized that I should share the information that I needed when I was in the midst of my doctoral program with the aim of equipping you to consciously choose to invest in your own success rather than that of your oppressor.

Be Yourself

I attended one of the finest Jesuit Universities in the United States. The faculty was filled with Professors who were well qualified and showed a genuine love for teaching and for students. My classmates were some of the finest nerds from across the land. Each week, I was impressed by their stories and experiences. I continue to be impressed by them and I am done with school. There was a part of me that wanted to be like them. I wanted to wax poetically about Friere or be able to stand before the class, with little preparation, and go on and on about the latest in the literature. That was not my calling. I am who I am and truly that is enough.

As you progress through your doctoral program, know that you are not out of place. You belong there. There may be those who play the "academic" game better, but you have other skills. Make a list of those skills, just in case you need a reminder. Imposter syndrome is real, but you are the real deal. There were times that I felt like

I was faking my way through. I know that I was not alone in this. My authentic self was made to succeed in every room entered. The classroom and boardrooms were not exempt.

Know Yourself

The very nature of the school is made for children, even in graduate programs that claim to be created for working adults. As a graduate student, it was the norm to be assigned a whole book to read and a paper to write for a single class, due in the next class session. This workload did not take into account competing priorities; an adult with a full-time job, children, and/or other caregiving responsibilities. I made it through and you can too. As a Black woman, I made magic happen so often that I forgot that I held creative power.

I made magic in the midst of real life. An adult in a doctoral program, I become adept at walking circumspectly between competing responsibilities—home, work, and school. Real life, however, caused my Black Girl Magic to go into overdrive. I joke by personifying "real life" as female. She has an attitude and is neither a woman nor a lady, she is a Bitch, even, and her motto is "I brought you in this world and I will take you out." Real life will come in the form of things over which you have no control—a sick child, a sick parent, natural disaster, and mass job layoff. When real life came for me, suddenly, graduate school felt like an expensive vanity project that was of no use, competing against the "real life" issues that I was facing. I wish I could tell you that she would let you postpone her arrival until a better time but it doesn't work that way. I had to learn to manage, survive, even in her midst. Sometimes that meant working harder to finish quicker; other times it meant taking a short purposeful pause. It also meant learning to manage my resources (family, friends, and money) in order to complete the doctoral program and ensure that the most important things ("real life") were handled properly. Although school was no match for "real life" it came with its own set of challenges.

Guard Yourself

A friend of mine in the program always said that "the dissertation process is toxic." It is the nature of the design. At different points along the way, I thought that it was me. And while you are in the dissertation process, you may believe that it is you. It is not, it is the process. The experience you have in the process will depend on your committee. Early on I made a mistake, rather a conscious choice to write my dissertation for my committee just to get through it. This made the whole process harder. It is like doing somebody else's homework—which I don't recommend. The end result is trying to create a story you want to tell but blocking your own progress. In the end, I did not like the product I put months of work into completing. If I had retained ownership, it would have been a much better finished product and the process would have been less debilitating.

The process was very draining mentally and intellectually. I spent my life not being swayed by others opinions of me—I alone defined myself. And I was voluntarily entering a process where every step I chose was judged by others whose opinions on my choices dictated my movement through the process. This was counterintuitive to how I had lived my life prior to graduate studies. With fight or flight being my only options, I fought. That's right, I fought against myself and a choice I had made. Learn from me, retain ownership of your process. Your dissertation may not be your life's work but it is your work just the same. So, even in a process that is toxic by design, own your work and articulate your vision. Entertain advice but still write *your* dissertation. Separate personal opinion from substantive advice. Knowing yourself leads to trusting yourself. Your opinion is the only one that actually matters from choosing your topic to how you present your research—own it.

Trust Yourself

Choose your topic wisely. Ensure it is something that will hold your interest in the research process. Ensure that the data you will need is available. I picked a topic that everybody had an opinion about and that presented new challenges. As I delved deeper into my topic, I was challenged by the critics who sought to usurp my authority by turning my story into their own. I selected a topic that was so personal that it felt as if I was being asked to dissect how my Grandmother lived her life and her choices. If I had surmised earlier that my topic was too personal; I could have made adjustments to transition to a topic where I would not have been so vulnerable. Imagine making this realization in the defense phase, like I did. The personal is better suited for your life's work. I am not suggesting that a personal topic should not be used for your dissertation; however, be sure that the topic is something that you would feel comfortable having critiqued.

In reflection, the most profitable information I can share is that you "were saved for such a time like this" (KJV, Esther 4:14). Everything that you have experienced up until this point, has been preparing you for this moment. It is a great challenge but you are up for it. In this time of turmoil and strife, I cannot be silent and neither can you. We are each endowed with the power to effect change, in small and grand ways, all equally important. Use your power, your way. Trust that you can make a difference. As you come to the end of the arduous doctoral journey, the world will be open to you. Be brave. Use your gifts to improve lives. Those roadblocks that will be placed in your path are really stepping stones. You are able to overcome them. Stand tall. I know it sounds like an empty platitude; except, I have been there.

As I was finishing my doctoral program, "real life" came for me hard. I had all these things that were happening in my life over which I had no control. My parents were suddenly ill, and in the midst of final revisions, my father passed away. I was spectacularly unprepared. Suddenly, the last revisions that seemed like a minor task were equal to a climb up Mt. Everest while carrying a sofa on my back. My head that had been filled with facts from my research, was now overflowing with grief. I had to use my resources (in this instance, it was my Black Girl Magic Crew that supported me throughout the dissertation process) to get back on track and complete the revisions. I got it done. And I am now a Whole Entire Doctor. If I can get it done, so can you. Surround yourself with a friend or two, who will let you vent and then say "now get your butt back to work." If "real life" comes for you during the process, manage her and keep pressing forward. This is your time. You can do it. Nobody is better at being you, than you. You too, can be a Whole Entire Doctor.

Part II

Curating Community

What's interesting? What's relevant? and Why do we care? are questions that curators pose. Each vignette in this section describes a curated community, roles that members of communities have played, and how people of color have forged ahead as a result of these relationships. By curating community people of color create support systems—tribes, clans, families, comprised of friends, family, colleagues, mentors, and others. Curated communities are needed to generate a space where the production of voice, visibility, and self-definition flourishes and in turn informs advocacy and activism for the entire community.

Curating a community involves weeding through your contacts and associations to find the best resources—those that exceed all others and offer the most good. Curated communities allow participants to fully embrace everyday living encompassed by the ability to sit with the realities that are present in historical, political, social, and sacred spheres. This form of fellowship involves sourcing information in new ways and delivering that knowledge to others in the community. By understanding the depth of one's history, the curator and the community, who are one in the same, constantly evolve into their best selves by participating in the ritual of call and response determining the importance of the place and the people present.

In this regard the community members are natural curators who create aggregated content as well as systematically organize (mashup) it for recall or research as needed all while determining its importance based on what happens in real time. Both curating a community and community curation activities are experiential in nature involving all your senses. The vignettes in this section evince how people of color curated their community.

10 The Journey

Bridget H. Love

An athlete in my youth I am familiar with conditioning. I was a runner, not particularly fast or skilled but a runner nonetheless. I remember the countless hours spent on calisthenics including but not limited to warming up muscles, stretching, and simple repeated drills.

Burpees were not my friends.

The days of "practice" after a full day of classes seemed long and arduous. In retrospect, I see how I benefited from more than just the physicality of practice but also the life discipline it created. A few years ago, I decided to again take up running. I was always taught to train for something. So, with that in mind I set my sights on running the Oakland marathon. Years had passed, pounds were added, and physical injuries occurred since I last trained for something like this. I was determined to run the 5K. You did not think that I was going to run the full 26.2 mile marathon, did you?

Studies show that people who write their goals down and make a realistic plan with actionable steps are successful in reaching them. I am relatively successful, I thought. I won't be punked so I registered for the race and downloaded an app on my phone. Might I digress here—no one forced me to run. There were no external influences that demanded that I do it. Yet I was compelled. Philippians 3:12 describes it this way, "I keep on running and struggling to take hold of the prize. I don't feel that I have already arrived. But I forget what is behind, and I struggle for what is ahead. I run toward the goal, so that I can win the prize." This was my goal and mine alone. I set my eyes on the prize. No one trained with me. Even my besties said that they would support me, albeit from the sidelines. I downloaded an app whose creators said would move you from walking to running in eight weeks.

I had to walk before I could run—literally.

The race was six months away and I had not run in over 20 years. Like any person given to administration and process I pulled out some paper and charted my course to the finish line. I drafted my running schedule and even solicited help from a dietician to make sure that I would be ready. I invested in my own success—I bought new, good running/cross-training shoes and moisture-wicking attire. There was more junk in my trunk than when I ran the last time, but I was committed. The running app had you run a minute and then walk the next for 30 minutes at a time. Depending on how comfortable you were you could move to the next session: run 2 minutes and walk 1 minute. This cycle continued until your running time was fluid. Conditioning for the average person was supposed to take eight weeks. Not for me. I was walking until I ran the actual 5K six months later, but I finished.

While you may not be training for a marathon or anything at all athletic you will have opportunities to embark on something new, whether it is a new degree, or a new venture. The lesson: Remember the journey. Each day is a new day that holds the potential to excite, enliven, and inspire you. Even the seemingly mundane activities not only get you closer to accomplishing long-term goals but also develop character, consistency, and courage. Why do I say courage? It takes courage to be a Black person in America. Courage to dare to live in confined spaces and choose to celebrate yourself and others just for being alive. It takes courage to reimagine a world that is inclusive not just in word but also in deed.

Though the journey may be longer than you anticipate or with terrain that was unexpected it does have hidden treasures that are yours for the taking. There was a lot of time invested leading up to the race. The race itself was only 1–5 hours for the fastest participant to the slowest. We all have one thing in common—we finished. At the end of this chapter, I will share with you some of the lessons that I learned while on the run that did not happen while I trained but were as much a part of the process and my success as a runner.

Remember, I am a runner and a planner who has huge issues with control and scheduling. When I decided to go to graduate school, I attacked the application matriculation processes the same way I trained to run. I found an app and mapped out all of the components that I would need to finish. Instead of run-walking my way into graduate school I was immigrating from one culture to another. Much like immigrants who traverse unbearable terrains in search of a better life I too sought something. In the search I found myself—a hidden treasure to behold. Like you and many others my educational "immigration" was consistent with immigrants from all over the world who go through the four stages: excitement, culture shock, gradual recovery, and full recovery.

Step 1: Excitement—The Honeymoon Stage

Upon first arriving across the bridge to the new culture, a doctoral program, I was excited about the opportunity to learn and participate in a community of practice of emerging scholars. My curiosity was stimulated by the discourses that I heard in the annals. The fact that I could just be a student addressing issues of race and culture was a novel idea. So novel, that it worked on my amygdala to create a sense of euphoria. I felt relatively connected to my homeland (predoctoral past) and would return nightly after class to decompress and release the experiences of the day abroad.

Step 2: Culture Shock

A little later, I realized that my newly acquired knowledge and even desire to learn at this level created a chasm of difference in my homeland. I experienced culture shock. Culture shock can be characterized by periods of frustration, adjustment, and even depression. Culture shock is the emotional and sometimes even physical discomfort we feel when we must leave everything familiar behind and find our way in a new culture that has a different way of life.

My extraneous cognitive load became negatively impacted as I worked to manage both the culture of my past with that of my present as they intersected inside me. Where I once felt secure and focused, I began having doubts, often felt incompetent unsure, and isolated (aka Imposters Syndrome). People from my past who used to be sources of support and comfort could no longer relate to my journey to scholarship. My intellectual pursuit and growth had surpassed their accomplishments leaving me alone in uncharted waters.

This is not the end of my story but rather an opportunity to locate the hidden treasure of choice. I decided to live in the ampersand: no longer "this" or "that" but the "and". Yes, you can have it all. Having it all does take some work. It took scheduling, connecting with other ampersand livers and continuing onward despite the opposition of those who were comfortable with having me boxed in.

Step 3: Gradual Recovery

Breaking free was no easy feat. There were times when I thought that I had broken free just to realize that the chains of my captors were just laxed a little. My captors were intellectual and emotional bonds of self-doubt, internalized racism, and sexism. Feeling frustrated yet determined to press forward, I reached for the Afrocentric worldview that includes spirituality at its core. I sang my own version of Frozen's "Let It Go" and reached forward.

Working through anger and frustration, and even environmental hostility at times, I questioned why I chose this pursuit at this time in my life and reminisced about what it was like before I was working full time, going to school in the evenings, and staying up late to either read or write papers. Comparing what was familiar to what I was coming to know did not bring me comfort in a dichotomized space that was unable to embrace my complexities. I felt like a fish out of water gasping for air. Leaning back to my spiritual practice, I focused my thoughts through the frame of the Bible scripture in Romans 8:28 that says "all things work together for my good." I was able to recalibrate my level of cognitive dissonance about the two worlds.

Step 4: Full Recovery

Instead of trying to fit in one world or the other, I learned to embrace my spanning identity. I was a bridge, a catalyst, an intersectional person who can go in and out of cultures. The scholar-practitioner that I became was not much different from the emerging scholar that I once was—or you may be now.

Gaining confidence and learning to appreciate the uniqueness of the positionality that came with being an intersector and boundary scanner, I encourage you to become comfortable and confident to make decisions based upon your own preferences and values.

If my present self could have a meaningful conversation with my emerging scholar self I would share some insights in hopes of sparing needless pain, misunderstanding, and disbelief. In reflection, I want to share a few thoughts with you, my friend, that you might glean from my realities and gain wisdom from my experiences. Ecclesiastes 9:11 states:

> Life Is Not Fair. The fastest runner does not always win the race; the strongest soldier does not always win the battle; wise

people don't always get the food; smart people don't always get the wealth; educated people don't always get the praise they deserve. When the time comes, bad things can happen to anyone!

We must rejuvenate to be productive. Don't be afraid to step back, take a moment, relax, refresh, and regroup. To everything there is a season and a purpose. For runners there are days of rest to allow the muscles time to heal and increase productivity. I don't know what your self-care will look like, but what I do know is that you will not reach your full potential or enjoy the journey of finding all the treasures that lay in wait without it.

It is not so much about the finish line as much as it is about the process. Gaining an advanced degree is hard and should be celebrated, respected, and even honored, but we often overlook the little lessons of self-discovery along the way while running for the goal. When I finally made it to the race and the starting gun sounded, the other runners and I began the race together. Certain people called pace setters were running in the race too. They donned brightly colored jerseys and were proven runners for setting paces like an 8-minute mile. Persons who had that goal were encouraged to keep up with the 8-minute mile pace setter to ensure that they too would meet that mark. I will tell you that much of that day was a blur as my muscles ached in tandem with my heartbeat. What I do remember though is my friends who came to my race, watched me run, handed me water along different straights to keep me hydrated, and the one friend who ran the last quarter mile with me providing encouragement to the finish line. Earning a doctoral degree was much like running that race. Sentimental by nature, I kept my racing bib as well as all my diplomas as trophies of the races that I have run. My time did not matter. What mattered is that I finished. What mattered is that I trained to run my race. What mattered is that I reached for water when I needed it. What mattered is that I had people in my corner willing to give up their Saturday to watch me culminate months of preparation. What ultimately mattered is that people showed up for me.

Through this writing I am endeavoring to show up for you through your own journey of self-discovery. As the Ghanaian concept of Sankofa symbolizes, I am reaching back to pull you forward. Consider me your pacesetter. Not that there's a specific time in which to complete your race, but just know from my example that you can. I have proven that you can, and I promise you that you can survive the downhill spiral and live. There is more strength and perseverance in you than you ever expected. I came this far by faith leaning on the Lord and others. The journey is not just a process, rather, it is a gift for you to unwrap. Run your own race. I am here with you, part of your curated community cheering you on.

11 Fitting in When You Stand Out

Jesse Moland Jr.

Whenever you think of a scholar or an academic, who comes to mind? Perform an image search using those terms and see how long it takes for you to be represented in the results. As a Black doctoral candidate, I did not have the time to sift and sort through the results until I found someone who looked like me. It would appear that my skin tone precluded my participation in the upper echelon of higher education. Academia, however, is longing for, even calling out to and actively seeking individuals from underrepresented groups—those who look like me—to join its ranks. Unfortunately, the problem of fitting in and finding a sense of belonging in many of these institutions can be too much for some nascent scholars of color. As in other realms of American society, there is a precarious balance between doing what is necessary to gain admittance and retaining one's uniqueness.

It is not uncommon to walk into a room of doctoral students, colleagues, or constituents, either at the beginning of a semester or at a conference, and spend a few frantic moments looking for a familiar face—that is a face of the same or similar hue—only to realize that you are alone. My classes typically began with a continental breakfast and opening session with all of the master's and doctoral students in attendance. I would arrive early, get a pastry, fruit, and water, and make my way into the meeting room. I would never sit in the front nor the back, as those are the two places where I would draw the most attention. While I was known by my dean and graduate chair, I did not have a connection with any other students. I got to the point where I would not even scan the room for a familiar face. I would simply get my things, find a seat, and stay to myself.

In those moments of uncertainty and trepidation, I had to remember that I was chosen to be there and needed no additional permission to occupy my seat. I might not have looked like the majority of students in the room, but I was supposed to be there and needed to act as such. As the semesters progressed, much like a young child who was forced to change schools, I began to make connections with people who would eventually become my friends. It was the commonality of our experiences, like our struggles in the introduction to doctoral writing course, situations that we faced in our jobs in the education sector, and even our quest for a new lunch spot, that began to break down the perceived barrier created by my skin color.

Alone in a Crowded Room

I often tell people that no one truly understands what it is like to be a doctoral candidate unless they have been a doctoral candidate. Even then, the experiences we face are as unique as our fingerprints. Although so much of our work is done in solitude, we do need camaraderie to help push us over the finish line. That is why finding individuals who are in the trenches with you (or who have made it to the other side) is so important. Eventually, I found people who had similar experiences and ambitions with whom I was able to connect. However, this prospect is made much more difficult when you perceive that your skin color is a barrier to creating these needed relationships. Far too many scholars of color are alone, even in crowded rooms, potentially diminishing their chances of completing their program.

There is comfort when you find someone with whom you have shared experiences, whether good or bad. The majority of my classmates were in the field of education and had served in an administrative capacity as I had. The trials and tribulations that we faced transcended the physical distance between our schools and the cultural distance between us. These connections—not deep, intense friendships—were the beginning of the elimination of my loneliness.

Scholars of color often miss the encouragement and validation that comes from fraternizing with fellow doctoral candidates because they find it challenging to connect with people with whom they do not have much in common, or worse yet, they are discriminated against and shunned within their department. Through events hosted by my department, such as our annual picnic, I was given the opportunity to interact with fellow candidates outside of the classroom which allowed me to connect with others. Faculty members also used these events to work in the room and engage with every student. It was difficult for me—almost impossible—to leave one of these events without having had a meaningful conversation with a member of the faculty or a fellow student.

For those whose programs are not as committed to diversity and inclusion as mine, do not ignore the importance of connecting with other doctoral candidates, even outside of one's department or program. While not a replacement for programs actively working to be inclusive, not only in who they admit but in their interactions with their candidates, networking via social media and other technology-based avenues can help scholars of color connect with fellow scholars and mitigate the feelings and actualities of being alone. I had several friends who were doctoral candidates at other universities with whom I regularly checked in and received encouragement.

Perhaps it is a result of my introverted nature or a survival tactic that I developed over the years, but I am not dissuaded by being the only person of color in the room. Admittedly, it can be uncomfortable to have the attention of everyone on you and unnerving to see the puzzled and judgmental look on the faces of people wondering who you are and what you are doing there. Notwithstanding these feelings and perceptions, I know why I am in the room, what I have to do, and what I have to offer. This gives me the resolve—and the pride—to hold my head high and work alone, even in a crowd. While it is unfortunate that many scholars of color will have to face this, it is imperative that you become comfortable with being uncomfortable until your perception shifts.

Being comfortable with being alone in a crowded room is more about coming to the realization that you have a job to do, regardless of how you are received. I was assured of who I was and understood that no one else in the room was responsible for me achieving my goal. While it would have been great to walk in and immediately connect with others, that experience was not the priority.

You Have Been Chosen

All too often, we encounter people who question our presence in academia simply because of our skin color. Whether it is a look of bewilderment when you enter the room or getting asked questions that no one else gets asked, the implication is that you do not belong. While I did not perceive any such feelings from my professors, I was cognizant of the fact that I did not look like all of the other students, I had to remind myself that I completed an application and was accepted into my program. Now was not the time to question whether I was accepted because of my well-written application letter or because of my ethnicity, nor is it the time for you to question the same about why you were chosen. Although it may be true that some were chosen to increase departmental diversification, what matters is that the admission committee chose us. With all of the pressure on graduate programs to continue to churn out successful candidates, they carry the burden of selecting individuals that they are confident can withstand the rigors of graduate study. We belong in academia, and that cannot be taken away from us.

I was fortunate to be welcomed into my program and have a sense of belonging from the beginning. My program placed a high priority on ethnic diversity and had a large number of international students, including a large number of students from countries in Africa. While our skin color was the same, our experiences were not. We were scholars of color, but the frame of reference the international students had shaped by their shorter time in the United States gave them a more forgiving view of and different perspectives on things such as educational inequities and the lingering effects of slavery. Ultimately, the similar hue of our skin connected us and enabled us to learn from each other.

There were still moments when I questioned my place. Hearing a classmate or colleague speaking about their accomplishments in academia would always drop seeds of doubt into my mind. Even the thought of beginning my dissertation made me question if I was cut out for this journey. Thankfully, there were times when I would have professors validate my work, not just personally, but in front of an entire class and even in front of other faculty members. I viewed these professors as supporters of me and my efforts and they became essential members of my community. It even got to the point that professors would email me to check up on me if they had not seen me in a while. These experiences, affirming my work and my presence, confirmed that I did belong, not only in the program but in academia. People who I looked up to were sharing my work and having positive conversations about me when I was not present. Unfortunately, this is not the case for everyone, so learn not to overlook any positive comment, even if it is a backhanded compliment or veiled in discriminatory undertones. You must be convinced that you do belong—take responsibility for your mental well-being and be your own biggest supporter.

Learn to focus on the positive and compartmentalize the negative. A semester-long battle with one professor transformed my scholarly writing and made my dissertation flow. Had I taken her questions and sharp responses personally, I never would have gained as much as I did from her. In part, my connection with others in the class showed me that I was not being singled out, but that everyone was having similar struggles. I made the choice to grow from the situation rather than be defeated. It was something that I had to go through, so I decided to emerge from it better.

Breaking Stereotypes

My support system slowly grew as I matriculated through the program. I realized that students who had similar work experiences, students who had the same skin color, and professors who recognized the quality of my work were vital connections. Through it all, I also had family members that were fully supportive of my studies. With a thriving support system, I wish I could tell you that the journey got easier, but being supported does not prevent stereotypes from surfacing. Whether it was a microaggressor commenting on how well I spoke for a person of color or the assumption that I was an international student because of my skin color, stereotypes serve as one more barrier between you and the completion of your goal. While some would argue that it is best to ignore stereotypes and those who express them, the reality of the effects of these stereotypes must not be discounted.

Take comfort in the knowledge that you are not responsible for debunking all stereotypes associated with your ethnicity. I never set out to change, or even add to, the narrative surrounding scholars of color at my institution. My goal was simply to be the best that I could be in every situation and in performing every task. It was not my role to be the model Black male student. In the same way, you are not responsible for eliminating all of the stereotypes which have been assigned to you as an individual. As you continue along your journey and complete the tasks which you are given, you will find stereotypes falling on their own. There is no reason for you to add the weight of confronting all of the stereotypes people of color face daily to your workload.

Guarding Your Community

I never confuse what I do with who I am. It is possible to become so wrapped up in your doctoral work that you begin to draw your identity from how others respond to and judge your work. Take care, as the criticisms of others may be influenced by their misguided and bigoted perceptions. If you internalize these critiques instead of examining their veracity as it relates to your work, you run the risk of assuming a false identity rooted in the hate of another. You must be secure in knowing who you are independent of your work. I may never have another article published or contribute anything of significance to my field. That does not change the fact that I am still a husband, a son, a friend, and so much more. My experiences in academia do not define who I am but are a part of what I have chosen to do. Who I am will endure while what I do will pass away.

Our dissertations contain an acknowledgment section in which we recognize and honor all of those who we feel contributed to our achievements. These individuals may not have been with us during the entire journey, but we could identify at least one significant moment where their support was felt. They exemplify and represent our community. I often think of a community as a large group of people in the same area, when, in reality, the members of a community are those who have something in common. Ecclesiastes 4:12 states:

> By yourself you're unprotected. With a friend you can face the worst. Can you round up a third? A three-stranded rope isn't easily snapped.

It could be an experience, a class, a research interest, or an objective that binds people together. While you may stick out everywhere that you go and you may feel that you are alone, take courage in the fact that you are a member of a community of others who look like you. They, too, were alone and faced unimaginable injustices—but they made it, and you will too.

12 Empowered and Equipped
The Gift of Community

Janise Parker

Early Life Experiences: Silencing My Voice

Graduate school was challenging for me because I constantly battled with sharing my voice as an emerging practitioner and scholar. Before I share the specific struggles I encountered during my doctoral studies, it is important to understand my childhood upbringing and grade-school experiences to provide a context for my story. I was born and raised in the deep south where my mother frequently prepared my sister and me to navigate the realities of being a person of color in professional spaces primarily occupied by White individuals. She often told us to be mindful of how we presented ourselves in the company of others because opportunities were more likely to be taken away from people of color if others did not agree with our point of view. Consequently, I was cautious about what I said in the presence of White individuals, especially when my perspective challenged theirs. Essentially, I chose to keep my thoughts to myself more often than not due to what I perceived as self-protection.

Identified as a gifted student early in my grade-school career, I was used to occupying "solo status" (being one of a few minoritized individuals) in predominantly White educational spaces. Because I was tracked into more advanced classes, I was often the only minoritized student (or one of a few) in my classes, even when I attended schools that were relatively diverse. By the time I started my graduate program, I was accustomed to feeling ostracized by my White peers because my disposition, lived experiences, and perspectives were apparently different. I decided to cope with the feeling of social isolation that comes with having a unique perspective in the company of White individuals by silencing my voice—to refrain from making the dominant culture feel uncomfortable and avoid feeling rejected by them.

My mother's teachings and early experiences as the only person of color in educational spaces were relevant to my experiences in graduate school and the internal battle I constantly endured. Namely, refraining from contributing to class discussions and expressing my beliefs when completing written assignments, because I often thought about my mother's words and the social isolation I felt during my time in grade-school. I quickly learned that it was vital for me to share my perspective and challenge the status quo as an emerging professional in the field of education. Thus, I experienced significant stress, worrying constantly, during the first two years of my graduate program due to the tension I felt as a result of being hesitant to communicate my thoughts while longing to express my views. After engaging in intense self-reflection, I realized that silencing my voice interfered with what I desired to accomplish as an intellectual thinker and advocate for African American Kindergarten through 12th-grade students. I knew I needed confidence, assurance, and guidance to overcome my fears of missed opportunities and social rejection; and the support I found during my graduate studies empowered me to embrace and share my voice.

Graduate School: Embracing My Voice

Many of my negative experiences in graduate school occurred within the context of attempting to develop genuine relationships with my White peers. Unfortunately, I was not always invited to social gatherings; my input in class was sometimes scoffed at by my White peers; and I simply did not share the same views on key socio-political issues as my White peers. Furthermore, I was not satisfied with some of the content we were required to learn as budding professionals. Much of the information we learned about African American Kindergarten through 12th-grade students highlighted their educational challenges, with little to no discussion about the cultural strengths that educators could build upon to support African American youth in school. Contrary to the deficit-based content we were exposed to in our coursework, I strongly believed it was important to capitalize on internal and external sources of strength among African American Kindergarten through 12th-grade students to support them in a more holistic manner. Yet, I did not make my stance known during the early stages of my graduate training.

I wanted to express my concerns in class and share a more critical perspective in my writing assignments, but in the presence of people

I viewed as not having my back I did not feel comfortable articulating my thoughts. I continued silencing my voice and became tired and frustrated. As my coursework came to an end and I transitioned to dissertating conversations with my advisor about my post-graduate school plans (i.e., teaching and conducting research as a professor), I could no longer accept what I perceived as my display of cowardice behavior. I wanted to be heard, so I sought social support on and off campus to help me "push through the silence."

Confidence Gained: Support from My Church Community

Though I knew there was another "one of me" in my cohort (a Black identified woman), I felt alone and isolated because we were still getting to know each other. At the end of my first semester, I called my mother, cried, and expressed my desire to quit the program. She encouraged me to stay the course and to rely on our faith to see me through. Religion (defined as my commitment to worshiping with my faith community and participating in sacred rituals to honor our God) and spirituality (defined as my personal relationship with God) have always been a critical aspect of my identity. So, I did just what she said. I prayed often about my experience and I found comfort in being around all the African American men and women who were members of a local church that I joined. As a youth leader, I watched the youth exhibit spiritual, emotional, and academic growth. The youth learned how to overcome everyday adversities, such as dealing with school-based bullying, in our Bible studies and bi-weekly meetings, they gave back to their community through mission-work and service and received tutoring. I enjoyed mentoring Black youth in my faith community and beyond providing emotional and social support. In addition to supporting the youth at my church, I received encouragement from the church elders who often affirmed my work as a youth leader. When I communicated my struggles at school my pastors prayed for me. One of them even made it a point to remind me that my commitment to working with marginalized youth was a reflection of me following the vision that God put on my heart, so I should not allow my fears to hold me back. By offering prayer and verbal encouragement, the members of my church community served as my support system outside of my graduate program. My experience as a youth leader gave me the confidence I needed to begin to let my voice be heard and champion for a strengths-based approach to supporting African American youth.

Words of Assurance: Support from My Black Identified Peer

As time went on, the other Black identified woman in my program and I began to form a genuine friendship. We studied together, supported one another, and often expressed our frustrations about the climate we encountered. I admired the courage she displayed when she assertively challenged systems of power. Inspired by her humble boldness and drawing from the confidence I gained through my religious community, I began to let my voice be heard. I expressed my views in a more subtle manner during class discussions, such as using Socratic questioning to get my point across and "dropping" nuggets of knowledge here and there versus "letting it all out" at once. Although this way of operating felt natural for me, I often wondered whether I was *finally* doing the right thing by letting my voice be heard or continuing to display cowardice behavior. The other Black identified woman was more direct in her approach, so there were several times when I felt like a "sell out," as if I was turning my back on other people of color, because I did not confront questionable perspectives directly.

After having several conversations with my new friend to determine whether my approach was right or wrong, she affirmed who I was and encouraged me to stay true to myself. We often reminded each other that the world needed both Malcom X and Dr. Martin Luther King, Jr.: two solutions to the same problem. Even though our approach to sharing our perspectives was different and we both engaged in our own individual ways of coping to deal with the frustration we experienced, we eventually found solace in each other as well. We were willing to learn from one another, and most importantly, we comforted each other when we needed it most. Overall, I am thankful for her support because she helped me embrace my voice and maintain the courage to use it in a manner that was authentic to me.

Mentorship and Guidance: Support from a Faculty of Color

Finally, the mentorship I gained from a faculty of color on campus helped me learn to communicate my voice through scholarly writing. Because she worked in a similar field of study, she understood the needs of African American youth, and her scholarship reflected her commitment to improve research and practice relative to serving marginalized youth. She also understood the politics that came with challenging the status quo as a graduate student of color immersed in predominantly White institutions. Thus, like my mother, this professor reminded me to be careful about what I communicated in class and in my written course assignments. Unlike my mother (who did not understand the world of academia), however, this professor coupled her words of caution with guidance. She taught me how to frame my thoughts in a scholarly manner, especially through my academic writing. She also taught me how to challenge the status quo as an academic by being intentional about where I seek to publish my research. For example, when discussing my desire to draft a paper about supporting Black high school males, she emphasized the importance of targeting professional journals that likely had a large following from White individuals as opposed to solely publishing in multicultural related journals.

Upon the end of my graduate studies, this professor was integral in helping me learn how to navigate the world of academia. The tips and strategies she shared served as a meaningful source of guidance, and I continue to apply the lessons she taught me as an Assistant Professor. As I began to think about my own research agenda upon transitioning from student to professor, our talks gave me a sense of direction as we discussed how I could build upon my dissertation in my professional career. Overall, she understood how to navigate the world of academia as a woman of color and the wisdom I gained from her helped me learn how to express my voice in a way that was most effective to increase the likelihood that White individuals would listen to my perspective.

What My Community Gave Me: Sharing My Voice

I attribute my growth in graduate school and beyond to the support I received during my five years of graduate training. My church family helped build my confidence by praying for me, allowing me to gain "real world" experience related to my views about supporting marginalized youth (i.e., supporting them from a strength-based perspective), and encouraging me to continue in my efforts to advocate for African American youth. The other Black identified woman in my graduate cohort affirmed my approach to expressing my views by assuring me that my more subtle method of challenging systems of oppression was just as valuable as the use of a more direct approach, which aligned with her method of professional confrontation. Last, the mentorship I gained from a faculty of color helped me navigate my graduate studies successfully (i.e., writing as a scholar in the academy) and prepare for life after graduation. I am thankful for the people I encountered in and outside of school, as they empowered me to continue to share my voice in professional spaces primarily occupied by White individuals.

13 A Syncopated Scholarly Journey

The Rhythm and Rhyme to Keep On Moving

Verna Orr

In August 2015, I joined the Educational Policy, Organizational & Leadership (EPOL) program in the College of Education at the University of Illinois Urbana Champaign (UIUC) with a higher education concentration. At the same time, I began a graduate assistantship at the National Institute for Learning Outcomes Assessment (NILOA), a research and resource development organization, which came with a tuition waiver and monthly stipend to cover my living expenses. Throughout my time at UIUC and NILOA, I challenged the narrative on equity in education while simultaneously critiquing, grappling with, and finally accepting the fact that academe is saturated with messy, conflicting, and syncopated messages; albeit necessary in my pursuit of agency, freedom, and peace as a Black woman researcher.

UIUC changed me. This University in midwestern America contributed to a heightened awareness of the systematic syncopated pulse of competing forms of domination in higher education. My previous higher education experience—as a student and staff member at a historically Black institution (HBCU) shielded me from oppressive subtleties that never tire at my predominantly White institution (PWI). I like to say my previous experiences served as my unbowed, unconquerable foundation in this foreign land called "the academy." Syncopation—a disturbance or interruption of the regular rhythm, a placement of rhythmic stresses or accents where they wouldn't normally occur. A temporary displacement of the regular metrical accent caused by stressing the weak beat.

Keep on Moving: My Reason, Rhythm, and Rhyme

I am often asked why in the world would I pursue a second doctoral degree? Depending on the day, how I am feeling, and who I am talking to, my answer varies. Some think I might have naively drunk from the cup of artificial sweetener that contributes to the legacy of exclusion and elitism, that is the higher education system. As I reflect and exert my power in this space, I say, I chose this path because the academy oftentimes excludes Black women—not our ideas, but our names, stories, and research. For too long, the major contributions of Black women scholars have been dressed up as regurgitated "scholarship" which has shifted the conversation from Black women being producers of knowledge to consumers of the same. Thus, my reason, rhythm, and rhyme was my community of Black women scholars who provided support, balance, counsel, friendship, and mentorship. Finding this sisterly community was what I needed to keep on moving.

I am grateful for the opportunity to indulge in this transformative truth-telling work. I found my community and found a way out of the beautiful struggle which increased my understanding of who I am, my space in the academy, and my obligation to Black women who are preparing for their own journeys. Herein lies the rhythm and rhyme that kept my feet in step.

Authenticity

I graduated from a performing arts high school in Jacksonville, Florida, and received a Bachelor of Music Education from Howard University in 2000. My love and respect for the sincerity of music began in the church. As a lifetime member of the Church of Christ, a cappella singing is a prominent part of worship service—that is, creating a melody without the use of instrumental accompaniment. Hence, I was pushed to train my ear (and heart) to hear what was not there. Having a performing arts background impacted my approach and way of knowing. I am able to enjoy a full experience, guided by imagination, free from assumption.

When I enrolled in the EPOL program at UIUC, I was a nontraditional student with more than 15 years of work experience. I come from a solid, active Christian, working-class Black family. My parents (like so many others) sacrificed and worked hard to ensure that their children had choices in life. Contrary to popular belief, there are Black people who come from families and communities that are involved, community leaders, change-makers, and connoisseurs of the arts.

Needless to say, I was confident in my abilities to succeed and excel in my higher education PhD program. I mean, I graduated from Howard University, "The Mecca!" I was ready for the work. My cohort members included recent college graduates and more seasoned folks, like me. Some had work experiences, some had families, some were legacy admits, others of us were admitted by our own merit. Living in a small, mostly White, cornfield-filled, college town, revealed our association with and understanding of the higher education system. Regardless of how we were admitted or what we chose to study (from finance to administration to law and everything in between), the rhythmless rhyme of a journey had begun.

Intentionality

I would consider myself a lifelong student with four degrees; a bachelor's, master's, and two doctorate degrees. And despite my background, educational experiences, and unconquerable foundation, I was oftentimes floored by my experiences at UIUC. The race dynamic was acted out in every interaction; from course "discussions" where I, along with other Black students, had to teach professors how to properly address race, to silence from cohort members when race entered a discussion. It was draining to know that some professors had no clue on how to handle issues of race, or worse, seemed to not care, but I found comfort in my community's insistence on my greatness. To be clear, I formed relationships with well-meaning, sincere people—across all disciplines and races, however, there was a community of Black women that kept my mind and spirit pure.

My storied lesson began in late fall of 2015, when I found myself in a sort of emotional turmoil where I struggled with the questions: *What is scholarly?* and *What do I know to be true?* Having been a student leader, scholar, and musician with the luxury of intrusive mentors, I suddenly found myself in a power struggle with the academy. I declared my victory by intentionally approaching my scholarly journey guided by imagination and free from assumption. With guidance from mentors and sister scholars I used scholarship to keep my feet in step: I learned to dig deeply into the annals of Black education history and call upon the wisdom of those who prayed for and paved a way for me. I learned that our lived experiences are deserving of scholarly inquiry. Intentionality coupled with authenticity made room for me.

Community Matters

For some of my cohort members, our shared midwestern university contributed to a heightened awareness of being at the crossroads of competing forms of oppression in higher education. For others, their university was and remains, a safe space that has grown, groomed, and granted access to possibilities unlimited. The intersections of race, class, gender, sex, and all other isms, proved to be the interference that perpetuated a lingering legacy of subjugation that legitimized "scholarship" in the academy. At UIUC, I quickly learned that authenticity, intentionality, and community are holy.

Truth-seeking scholarly inquiry can sometimes be a lonely place. However, my community sustained my right mind even in the most desperate times. The research community oftentimes ignore the authentic lived experiences of Black women in higher education, specifically, those pursuing terminal degrees. The erasure of Black women's scholarly journeys is literally deafening, although our influence is undeniable. Our work is regurgitated into a watered-down version of the truth. Plainly stated, the manner in which discriminatory systems coalesce to create inequities for Black women is real. My community of Black women scholars prepared a safe place for me. From celebrating small steps toward my goals to providing firm but fair critiques to literally praying for me in the middle of a crowded grocery store—my community loved me through the confusion.

They introduced me to Kimberle Crenshaw's intersectionality framework, which eloquently describes the manner in which structural oppression creates inequities for Black women that must be considered to fully understand its impact.

Keep on Moving, Don't Stop

My Gift

In April of 2018, I attended a dissertation defense that engaged artistic mediums for the purpose of Black girlhood celebration and freedom. Interestingly enough, the dissertation defense opened with a song—in celebration of grandmothers' prayers. This beautiful scholarly masterpiece centering Black girlhood was a revolutionary moment for me and a testament to Nikky Finney's idea of "courage being a daughter's name." To think, I had spent almost two years wrestling with the idea of suppressing the very thing that made me unique—my gift.

When I consider the past five and a half years, I confidently smile and know deeply that this journey was divinely ordered; it brought me back to myself. This radical act of being a free-thinking, confident, brilliant, Black woman scholar can be complicated.

However, my scholar-sister-friends (the thought interrupters) in the beautiful struggle at UIUC sustained me in an incredible, indescribable, irreplaceable way. It is important that we speak there names—#CiteASista in our scholarship, because it matters.

My community of sister scholars, proven tried and true, provided love and laughs even in times of great confusion. They challenged me to see more. They were everything I never knew I needed. In addition to these women, my parents provided ongoing anchoring. My community coupled with my indulgence of the research finds me, a scholar, unafraid. Unafraid to ask questions. Unafraid of critique. Unafraid to learn. Unafraid to grow. Unafraid to share. In retrospect, I found my rhythm and kept in step by the following.

1 Being authentic.
2 Recognizing that my community was greater than my University, and proceeding with caution whenever processes were not driven by love for people.
3 Remembering that I am gifted and my gifts make room for me.
4 Acknowledging sources of support; #CiteASista.
5 Knowing my why.

My sincere hope for you is that this chapter will evoke an unwavering commitment to authenticity, intentionality, self-care, equity, and our community. My hope is that our search for truth, light, and right will be the rhythm that will keep our feet in step. Never missing a beat. My community gave so much to me and my family, I am unsure if there are words to describe my appreciation. Be it not lost on me to encourage you to push the envelope and challenge the research community to see more, for better or worse. It is our duty as scholars, an obligation to our community, and a privilege, indeed. Onward family!

14 Writing to the Choir

The Imperative of Rest for Women of Color PhD Students

Jasmine Abukar

I am worried about my fellow women of color in graduate school. I am worried about the amount of labor that is expected of us and the burdens we choose to take on, but mostly, I am worried about the consequences of us doing the most. We need to rest.

I once attended a meeting at a community space for women of color. At the end of the meeting, our conversation organically turned to familiar territory: The burden of being the "only one," the pressure to excel in spite of the odds, and the fatigue of fighting systems of oppression. Those of us in academia shared how the unique pressures of higher education seemed to exacerbate these challenges. We wondered together when we would experience reprieve. Another PhD student described herself as "running on E" and coming down with a sudden cold. Only a few moments later, she excused herself to go to a late evening organizing meeting. Having just engaged in this powerful and cathartic discussion, I became exasperated with her behavior and asked if she valued her health. She responded quickly as she left, "Only the privileged can afford to take time off from liberation movements." Many around the room agreed with her, including me.

Still, I wondered: What happens to a movement full of martyrs? How can we enjoy the progress we have made, as little or great as it may be, if we never stop to look around? Why don't we have Calls to Rest along with Calls to Action? What would happen if we could bring our full, healthy selves to the causes we care so deeply about?

The palpable fatigue of my peers concerned me. I know the physical, emotional, and mental costs of resistance and overwork in daily life. In my undergraduate years, at the height of my activism and while I worked three jobs on top of school, I had frequent depressive episodes in which I barely left my bed for days at a time. The trend continued as I pursued my master's degree and worked as a graduate associate. By the time I reached two years of full-time work in academia, I was completely burnt out. Though I knew my passion was in higher education, I made the difficult choice to leave the field. It took a few years of working a nice, but not nearly as fulfilling nine-to-five job before I felt I could return to the academy to pursue a PhD. By that time, I was actively cultivating more balance in my life.

Yet, as many women of color in graduate school know all too well, the pursuit of a terminal degree can result in a wide range of mental, emotional, and physical ailments. While a mental health crisis has been established for graduate students in general, we face unique health challenges compared to our peers of other races and genders. So, the shared fatigue of my peers did not come as much of a surprise. Despite my renewed sense of balance and pleas for others to value their health, I sometimes found myself exhausted too.

As I sat exasperated in the community space, I looked around the room we were seated in and noticed a framed decorative poster displaying the words of feminist scholar and activist Audre Lorde: "Caring for myself is not self-indulgence, it is self-preservation, and that is an act of political warfare." There was a certain irony to the poster's prominent location in a space full of women of color who seemed to take pride in prioritizing nearly everything and everyone else over self-care. I decided that pointing to Lorde's words was not the best choice in the moment. Sometimes, people just need to vent.

The fatigue and irony present in the community space stayed with me for days. I sought out more information on Audre Lorde's words and found that she wrote about self-care as political warfare in her final years as she was grappling with the cancer diagnosis that would eventually cause her death. She ends her 1988 work *A Burst of Light: Essays*, with various notes and reflections on love, rest, health, and resistance, including the now-famous quote displayed on the poster. Within the same section of that quote, Lorde discussed the perilous consequences of overextension. This perilousness matched so much of what I felt in that conversation but not what was said. As we shared our stories, exclamations of "I'm tired!" and "There's just not enough hours in the day" were accompanied by a paradoxical satisfaction and exhaustion that I recognized.

How frequently had I taken pride in "doing it all?" How often did I list everything I was doing in casual conversations with friends? How many times had I used the excuse "If I don't sit on this committee, there won't be diverse representation?" When was the last time I had gone to bed peacefully and intentionally rather than collapsing in exhaustion? Perhaps I did not have as much balance as I thought. In fact, like many of my peers, I took pride in being busy.

One of the ways in which many women of color have internalized what bell hooks calls imperialist White supremacist capitalist patriarchy is by conflating our worth and legacy with our labor. The academy helps us in this conflation. As graduate students, we navigate the hidden curriculum, research, coursework, seemingly endless amounts of writing, and so much more. As women of color, we often carry the emotional and literal labor of educating our peers and faculty about our experiences while navigating racism, sexism, and other intersectional oppressions. We are in an environment where "publish or perish" is a common refrain. Naturally, my peers and I are proud of surviving this. But the pursuit of a PhD, while difficult, should not require survival skills.

Nonetheless, women of color in graduate school are engaging in political warfare, as Lorde described. Women of color are particularly susceptible to the violence and oppression of the academy. We fight against the interpersonal gendered racism of our colleagues while dismantling institutional oppression on our campuses. We combat the effects of vicarious trauma that reaches us via a 24/7 news cycle and social media. We fight for visibility, for justice, and for change. We should not stop fighting nor should we let the battle consume us. We can fight while rested, deliberate, and whole. We can love ourselves enough to change this narrative, to let go of the pressures of doing it all. We are enough, as we are, simply for existing in these spaces. Our research, our perspectives, and our presence is resistance.

Resistance can also come in the form of rest. Choosing napping over the constant need for production, taking long breaks from work, letting someone else lead the charge for change, and saying "no" are all ways to resist. Not only does rest rejuvenate us for the battle, but it can contribute to our overall wellness. When rest became a regular part of my routine, I grew in my self-efficacy and became better at reinforcing boundaries. I was able to show up for the things that mattered and discern what things did not deserve my energy. I felt healthier and more refreshed. Rest also helped me become a better scholar. My writing improved, I was more attentive to my teaching, and I was less overwhelmed by the academy.

As an emerging researcher, I am committed to illuminating how students with marginalized identities resist institutional oppression. In addition to the personal benefits, my revelations on rest also led to a scholarly outcome: A large shift in my intended research focus to the possibilities of rest for women of color in PhD programs. This area of scholarship is rooted in my own experience and is also inspired by the women around me. It serves as an homage to the work of other women of color like Audre Lorde, public intellectual Rachel Cargle, and Tricia Hersey of The Nap Ministry. When I first began to explore rest as a scholarly contribution, I shared this emerging thought with women of color faculty I admire. Their positive, visceral reactions to the idea solidified the importance of this work. I was met with loud yeses, stomping feet, closed eyes with raised arms, and hands over hearts. There was not only a demonstrable way I could connect this concept with experiential knowledge and existing scholarship, but there was a desire from women in my academic community. The ultimate confirmation happened when I told my advisor that I planned to scrap my previous dissertation idea in favor of exploring rest. He replied, "I can already feel that this is right for the powerful scholar you are and are becoming."

As I continue to develop my scholarly identity, I carry that day in the community space and Lorde's words with me. I do not want to be a person who prioritizes changing the academy, research, teaching, and service over my own needs. Prioritizing my own needs is, in fact, a part of the work. There is time for rest. I once heard a beautiful analogy for this. In a choir, the music sometimes requires singers to hold a note for longer than is possible. In these cases, individual singers will stop to breathe in staggered breaks while the choir carries on. This alternation honors both the individual's need for rest and the collective work the song requires. My hope for the upcoming generation of women of color in the academy is that we, too, can honor our need for rest, knowing that there is a choir of scholars to support us.

15 Finding My People and My People Finding Me

Angelina Nortey

I was raised in a Ghanaian household and the importance of community was deeply instilled in me. I believed that being connected to other people was needed to survive and be well. While I knew this, embarking on doctoral studies at a predominantly White institution in the Southeast region of the United States would test the extent to which I truly lived and believed in this, as a young adult.

Right out of my undergraduate studies, I was naïve about navigating graduate school, nevertheless a doctoral program. I trusted that I made a good decision and that my faculty advisor was the right fit. Unbeknownst to me, I was about to experience the most racism I had ever dealt with while also navigating political and social dynamics. Prior to my doctoral studies, I was convinced that I knew all about racism. I was an Africana Studies minor as an undergrad and I believed that this knowledge base was sufficient. However, my doctoral studies required me to re-define racism and more fully lean into perspectives that I initially thought were extreme, based on the covert and entrenched way that it manifested. Although I did not realize it at the time, I was learning how to successfully resolve the discrepancy between textbook knowledge and lived experience. The resolution included being able to acknowledge my emotional experience, being introduced to ways of navigating the academy by Black faculty, learning how to be supported by and supportive of my Black peers as well as learning to turn the emotional experience into scholarship.

Alone and Naïve

The first year of my program was a culture shock. Simply, coming from the Northeast to the Southeast was a very hard adjustment. The interpersonal interactions were different, the twang in the voice was unfamiliar to me, the pace of life was slower and I did not know anyone. Daily I wanted to return home, but could not admit that I was willing to forfeit a prestigious fellowship because I was having a hard time adjusting. I thought that if I acknowledged this I would be perceived as a weakness so I kept it to myself for a long time. I figured that if I pushed through, it would all be okay.

One of the glaring changes in my day-to-day life was the reality of having close interactions with a group of mostly White women. As an undergraduate student, I always found people who I identified with in large classes, took smaller classes with people who mostly looked like me or navigated alone. However, the small cohort format of graduate school did not leave much room for me to continue to operate in the academic setting in the ways I had previously. The classroom dynamic created a barrier for me because peer interactions were disingenuous, forced at times, and filled with competitive overtones. An interaction that stood out was when a White woman peer sent me a text message suggesting that I was favored by our White professor and requested that I help her with our final assignment. It became clear to me that this peer and likely the other students, were not attuned to the dissonance that I was battling to complete assignments, or the microaggressions that I was experiencing to show up and participate in class daily. In my program, I received constant feedback about the way and the rate at which I spoke. I became self-conscious and double guessed myself. I even noticed that I began to take long pauses when attempting to express an idea, until I changed the way I spoke in the classroom and around professors. I did this until graduation, when I realized that my change in diction was a way of disconnecting from my true voice. I also began to dislike the word "passionate." This word was usually included in a response I received from faculty when it was clear that they were either shocked or uncertain about a comment I made, usually about the maltreatment of Black people.

I survived my first year academically and was slowly starting to develop peer relationships that felt more authentic. I was slowly developing a connection with the other two people of color, but the interactions were primarily based around completing work. I had gotten somewhat involved in the Black graduate student organization and started finding ways to venture beyond the walls of my classes.

By the time my second year arrived, I was disillusioned. I had high hopes of becoming a culturally competent clinician. The description of the program and the interview process reassured me of this and I believed them. To my disappointment, this was simply not the case. Classes were taught from a deficit-based perspective; Black people were talked about like we were not sitting in the room, and ideologies that promoted Black inferiority were projected on screens, to name a few. My motivation declined. I handed in assignments late and put little effort into my tasks. I questioned whether I made a mistake picking my program and discipline. I was filled with much uncertainty. Despite this challenging start, I soon learned critical lessons from trusting faculty members about how to navigate the system of higher education.

Learning About Underground Railroad Work

It was when I met a Black professor at the college that my motivation started to increase. I was walking in the hall one day, after introducing a prospective Black graduate student to the college and we ran into each other. She introduced herself and asked me in a very motherly way, why she did not know me. Coyly, I responded that I did not know. She suggested I email her to set up a meeting, which I did and we met in her office shortly after. During the meeting, she asked about my experiences thus far and offered other gems for navigating the space and professors. She expressed strong concerns about very smart Black women who have been unsuccessful in matriculating through my program. As such, she provided explicit steps for me to follow to ensure that I would leave the program successfully, with a letter of recommendation from the core faculty.

Subsequently, she introduced me to the idea of doing "underground railroad work" as a way of surviving the doctoral process as a conscious Black woman. This was the idea of engaging in Black-centered work and building relationships that were not apparent to the outside. This framework encouraged me to pursue resources and build relationships outside of what was provided in my program. This professor, who is a mentor to this day, started me off by suggesting some readings from her own shelf. Reading relevant and historical literature far outside of my discipline kept me inspired.

I also spent time talking with Black faculty in various colleges and schools across campus, including Law and Counseling Psychology. Meeting with these faculty members was necessary to help sort and make clear my ideas, as well as give me direction. Most importantly, my conversations with them affirmed my perspective, lived experience, and aspirations. It was a breath of fresh air and an indicator to continue in the direction that I was going. Furthermore, interacting with various Black professors I learned who my allies were on campus, highlighting the important role that allies play in the process and helping me to identify how allies positioned themselves in the academic setting. It was through these interactions that I stopped feeling alone because I knew that I was supported, even if most of the support came from outside of my program. I can now look back and say that my "elders" were guiding me through the doctoral process. Support from faculty members satisfied missing academic and intellectual needs, which were also addressed from active engagement with my peers.

Creating Space for Myself and Others

Joining the Black graduate student organization was critical in my groundedness. In my second and third years, I served on the executive board and was actively involved in organizing events. The time spent and conversations had with Black graduate students across campus solidified the pervasiveness of racism. Despite our very different disciplines, everyone had a story about how their intellect and/or scholarship was devalued and their expression of Black thought was deemed somehow inappropriate for a higher education setting such as ours. It was because of these experiences that we organized events such as our own book clubs and times for us to collectively share our research ideas with Black faculty across campus. However, beyond the academic experiences that we shared, I appreciated the social refuge that I experienced with my peers. I was able to be myself and not the version that I presented in academic circles with non-Black peers and faculty. We attended homecoming events at local Historically Black College and Universities(HBCUs), watched TV at each other's houses, shared Sunday dinner together, worked out together, and randomly connected when our schedules permitted. With my Black graduate student peers, I could be intellectual, cultural, and social at the same time.

Within my program, I developed a relationship with another Black peer, who I had initially deemed as very different from myself. While we were both Black women, we were from different regions of the country, varied culturally and expressed our Blackness distinctively. Despite these differences, we had a shared experience in the program that brought us together. A time when our country was grappling with the Trayvon Martin incident, classmates' responses in a newly offered cultural diversity course led me to withdraw and refrain from speaking in class, especially about justice and race related issues. However, I had people in my class and in my program who "got it" with whom I could express my true ideas. To this day, one of these people was my Black woman cohort member, who I initially did not view as someone critical to my success. Without her support, I would not have made it through my program. She always granted me a space to vent and filter my thoughts so that I could effectively navigate professional interactions with the expected tact and adherence to the unwritten decorum of higher education. What started as a relationship based on academics, eventually grew into a very well-connected friendship. Peer support served as a necessary component of surviving graduate studies and self-affirmation.

Bringing Community with Me

The quieter I got in class, the louder I got in my papers, and ultimately in my dissertation. When I read my dissertation now, I am proud of myself for having the courage to integrate Black-centered theory, namely Womanist ideology, into a discipline that is inherently racist. A professor suggested to me that my work would not be publishable and if so, only in a book and not in a journal. While writing my dissertation, the same professor commented about me not being like "those Black people" I chose to write about and focus on in my work. Comments like these that make the idea of solidarity and community extremely important to me. It was through this process that I came to understand Brittany Cooper's concept of "eloquent rage," where she provides an intellectual framework for understanding Black woman's anger as an appropriate political response, to various layers of oppression rather than an emotional problem.

My community, though invisible to my doctoral program, was present in my sphere. If it were not for the combination of racialized experiences and support in the name of mentorship, organization, and friendship, I would not be the professional I am today. In all of these experiences, I learned: There are people waiting to integrate me into their community, the community can exist in places least expected, and that community can be created. Even when I may feel alone due to experience, I'll remember the words of Maya Angelou: "I come as one, but I stand as 10,000."

16 Mothers in My Academic Village

Ashley Carpenter

Even though I am only in my late 20s, my academic story began in 1937 with the birth of my grandmother. Growing up in the deep south, my grandmother lived under the hard economic times of the Great Depression, and the inhumane racial segregation of Jim Crow. Born into poverty and deprived of the opportunities afforded to her White colleagues, my grandmother beat the odds, cleared the social hurdles of her time, and earned a PhD in Education. She inspired me; therefore I consistently tried to follow in her footsteps, no matter how long or wide her strides were. Following her path, ultimately led me to pursue a doctorate in higher education. One of her most notable traits was her way with words. During childhood, I loved watching and hearing my grandmother speak, as I could visualize the phrases of eloquence flowing from her mouth. Yet, her most memorable adages were always parables. Her favorite proverb was "it takes a village to raise a child." I always found the phrase cliché and overused, but I embodied this parable's meaning as I navigated graduate school. This allegory was the underpinning of my educational success, particularly as I matriculated through the first semester of my doctoral program. At my predominantly White institution (PWI) I was the only Black woman in my cohort. In fact, I was the only person of color within my department's last two cohorts. I quickly realized that I needed to find a "village" in my educational spaces. Building a village in these pervasively White spaces was a vital component to the way I would be "raised" as an academic and scholar of color. There are stressors that all doctoral students face during their tenure, yet the marginalization of my identities and other students of color manifests differently because we exist in spaces historically not created for us to succeed.

My experiences at a land-grant public institution in the Northeast were not unusual, as they were ramifications of an engrained archive of marginalization. For example, the first Black person to receive a PhD from my graduate institution did not do so until 1935. There were some drastic institutional changes made in the last 85 years, however, the aspects of pervasive segregation still impact the ways Black doctoral students navigate these spaces (i.e., being in classrooms and not having instructors or classmates that look like us). And unfortunately, until the beginning of the 20th century, most graduate students that went to my institution were White, cisgendered men from the Northeast. As my institution tried to "diversify" its student body, diversity stemmed mostly from international students (i.e., Brazil, Japan, Turkey, China, and Mexico). Diversity posited from this angle, often left out the admission of domestic people of color—which is still indicative of the current number of graduate students of color (~16%). Fundamentally, the historical nature of this institution and the history of segregation impacted my environment and continues to affect the villages and communities of current domestic students of color. Yet, in light of this reality and lived experience, I sought to create a village that could consist of people that reminded me of my grandmother and her parables. There were several ways that I found this "village" in my academic space during my dissertation process.

As there were many steps in fostering my academic village, I desperately sought after a community that could provide wisdom similar to that of my grandmother. I intentionally pursued academic "family," that could serve as supportive mentors. Graduate students—particularly graduate students of color—can not survive the rigors of graduate school without mentorship and support from faculty. Often in graduate school, students of color experience more isolation and less access to mentors and role-models than their White peers. And even when students of color form mentoring relationships, they may not be provided the same quality of mentorship (i.e., resources, time spent with mentors, access to various social networks) as their White colleagues. In addition to the literature on mentoring for graduate students of color, I personally saw the benefit of having mentors with similar intersectional identities. I found that the connections I had with the same race and gender mentors were more helpful and authentic in developing my personal and career development. The conversations that I had with Black women faculty were composed of a similar notion of collectivism and cultural values. Yet to quote my grandmother, "not all skin folk is kinfolk." I conceptualized this parable and created an extensive network of mentors with differing races/ethnicities, genders, professions/fields, and formal/informal relationships who provided the social capital needed to navigate all situations that I encountered in graduate school.

Even though I argue the importance of having varied mentors to accommodate the multifaceted aspects of one's academic, personal, and professional development, I found that Black women were pivotal to my success. This was the most evident during my dissertation process. I had the incredible opportunity to have three Black women on my dissertation committee, who created a space for me to bring all my beliefs and identities into my scholarship. These women were my academic "mothers," and they shaped my learning, advocacy, and authenticity as a scholar. Having a dissertation committee composed solely of Black women was a unique privilege noting the low percentages of Black women faculty in the professoriate leading to an even smaller number of Black women that can serve as faculty mentors. Even if we further contextualize the experiences of Black women faculty, many are simultaneously working on promotion and tenure, while engaging in invisible labor and combating discrimination, racism, and microaggressions. The lack of faculty of color puts marginalized students at a disadvantage in finding mentors of similar cultures. Yet, through all of these barriers, I found them. And most importantly, I thrived because of them. Like my grandmother, these three Black women taught me valuable lessons through parables. The following sections are quotes from them that helped guide me through the dissertation process to graduation.

"I'm Not Going to Let You Embarrass Me"

When my dissertation chair said this to me, it initially made me feel inferior as I interpreted what she said in a pejorative way. Yet, there was some truth in what she stated. It is imperative to have someone on your committee that consistently keeps it real with you. Although I was instinctively defensive of her comment, I realized that her remark was coming from a place of caution. I was a reflection of her, and she was a reflection of me in this process. She was a stickler but she wanted to ensure that I could keep up the rigors of the field and to continuously push myself forward. Through her motivation, I worked to make her proud, but most importantly produce work that I could be proud of. Her parable taught me that it is essential to have someone on your committee that consistently keeps you accountable, and reminds you of your end goal.

"You Know Best—No One Knows This Work as Much as You"

My second committee member was a cheerleader. She was a sounding board to bounce "dumb" ideas off of, but did so through a guise of loving critique. I valued talking to my academic "mother" about my work and personal/social identities, as this helped me bring my full self into my scholarship. I am not saying that my committee members were my therapists (I do think every graduate student should have a therapist); however, I discerned the importance of having an advocate to support you through tough situations. I often find that students of color must employ higher levels of grit than their White peers if they want to achieve both in and out of the classroom. Like faculty of color during the tenure process, many minoritized students are academically surviving and thriving despite encounters of racism, discrimination, and microaggressions. Faculty and students of color, alike, require higher levels of physical and mental grit to navigate the systemic challenges of academia. As it is necessary to critique systems that reinforce students' necessity to demonstrate grit, it is crucial to have someone that can provide a sense of security amongst the pernicious aspects of graduate programs.

"This Sounds Interesting, But What Do You Actually Mean?"

My third committee member was an academic "mother" who asked tough questions. As my outside committee member, she brought a fresh perspective that unconventionally challenged my thinking. She consistently made inquiries about my citations, models, and theoretical frameworks. Her insight was helpful, as she encouraged me to think of my work holistically. She reminded me to step away from viewing the document as pages of disjointed chapters, but a narrative that told a whole story. This frame of thinking helped me center on my participant's voices and contextualize myself as a researcher. Her lens of thinking was particularly important during the latter stages of the dissertation phase. During the last semester of graduate school, my grandmother always said that "a good dissertation is a done dissertation." Yet it was essential for me to make sure that my work was thoughtful and complete. I appreciated my academic "mother" for challenging the way I thought, even when I was burnt out at the end. The most valuable lesson she taught me was to not get comfortable in my work and scholarship, as there is always still room to grow.

These three Black women taught me so many valuable lessons. Like my grandmother, their parables and mentorship helped form my graduate school experiences and ultimately shaped the way I successfully navigated the dissertation process. They were not just my dissertation committee members but "mothers" in my village. Like many other PWIs, my graduate institution was historically rooted in systemic exclusion, which impacted the experiences of students and faculty of color alike. Having a dissertation committee with women who were my same race and gender allowed me to be vulnerable and nurtured in an academic space that often required me to remain stoic and strong. Unfortunately, Black women have to showcase strength despite experiences of adversity, racism, and sexism in the academy. Even though the "Strong Black Woman" narrative is criticized for the praise (and expectation) of Black women to survive trauma, I survived because of them.

Each of my dissertation committee members brought a varied sense of themselves to my work, which ultimately allowed me to do the same. I learned that graduate students, particularly graduate women of color, must be creative in the ways we search for support and guidance. Most notably, the physical presence of having three Black women sit at the table as I presented my dissertation work was a visceral act of resistance. Academia is filled with White supremacy and historic hegemonic practices that attempt to discredit and dishonor the work of women of color. It was externally and intrinsically satisfying to have three Black women who have defied these odds, like my grandmother, reinforce me and push me toward academic success. Their actions taught me the importance of supporting my peers and colleagues toward success, particularly academic communities of color. I am part of the next group of students of Color restructuring the hierarchies of higher education who are committed to the wise words of my grandmother, endeavoring to, "lift as I climb."

17 Dancing Between Two Worlds

Lisa J. Price

Community, that place of deep connection that provides emotional, physical, and spiritual security that literally feeds one's soul on so many levels. More than that, community connections and involvement for African Americans has generationally made the difference between illness and health, success and failure, ignorance and knowledge, and yes, even life and death. Community for many African Americans has throughout time been sought out and even mandated by such events as the atrocities of slavery, the inhumane and defiling experiences perpetuated and falsely validated by Jim Crow segregation laws, the quest for justice and equality fueling the Civil Rights movement, and the deterioration of our families resulting from the crack epidemic of the '80s. Not all thrusts toward community for African Americans, however, have been motivated by loss and despair. Sometimes it is the uniting of a couple in marriage or the birth of a child. While at other times, it is the achievement of a "first," whether on a world stage or on a local, familial level. Whatever the case, community in some form or fashion has been a hallmark within the lives of most African Americans. I am no exception to this notion. Alice Walker, the author of the book *The Color Purple*, admonished generations to look closely as the present that was being constructed with a critical lens to ensure that it would be the future that they desired.

For me, community, which has taken on multiple constructs and compositions over time for different reasons, has been my lifeline, source of strength, squad of encouragement, and haven of rest. The first time my parents introduced me to those outside of our family who would be trusted participants in my upbringing was within our faith community. This first introduction was within not only the confines of our embraced expression of faith but also within one of our deepest cultural articulations of Blackness that has been deeply embedded in African American history for decades on end. While it was not explained to me that way, I eventually arrived at this definitional resting place as a result of the many ways within this ark of safety that I came to understand a good majority of our history, colloquial expressions, values, and traditions as a people.

It was in this community called "church" that I was exposed to forms of spoken word cadences intertwined with rhythmical and stylistic blends of music that were expressed through hand clapping, foot stomping, and soulful instrumentation ranging from man-made devices to God given vocals with anointed agility. It was here that the sometimes directive and at other times poetic and metaphorical Word of God became intertwined in the foundation of my understanding of the guiding principles of my community and ultimately, myself. It was in this locale that I encountered things that, to this day, speak to me at various times and in various ways bringing direction, comfort, strength, inquiry, peace, joy, and a deep sense of being loved. It was within this rich grouping that I experienced kinship connections that will forever cause me to question the saying that "blood is thicker than water" with respect to familial relatedness. It was within this *koinonia*, that deep and intimate communion with God, morphed into a sense of "home" as I experienced my first sense of fellowship and belonging.

While I have belonged to other lifelong communities, my academic community was one that was probably the most culturally, politically, spiritually, and ethnically diverse. That mix of realms added to the richness of my life and broadened my world view and simultaneously served to isolate me in some ways. My grade-school years afforded me the dual experience of urban life and academic rigor that was mutually sacrificial. My urban inspired educational experience was in a public school setting composed of a healthy mixture of African Americans, Latinos, and Asians. As such, I had many African American friends but in order to access the academic rigor that would support my destined matriculation, I had to enter the world of academic programs for gifted and talented (GATE) students. This meant spending weekdays at my high school that reflected my community but weekends and summers at a local, prestigious University studying among some of the brightest students in the area; of which very few looked like me. Not surprisingly, this dance between two worlds slowly led to a sense of not fully belonging to either group. My African American friends wanted me to succeed but somewhat distanced themselves so that I was not influenced by the vices of the time in which many of them were engaged. Simultaneously, my GATE colleagues interacted only during class; not inviting me into their daily worlds. Yes, dual citizenship can sometimes be segregating. Despite this happening, I have always craved some form of a Black academic community.

Though I marveled at my perception of lifelong friendships formed at Historically Black Colleges and Universities (HBCU) or the not easily broken sisterhood that Greek Life seems to forge, I opted not to attend a HBCU or pledge a sorority. Instead, I sought out the "best school" for my profession at the time, knowing that any possible circles primarily composed of African Americans would be few at my chosen University. It was at this University as an undergraduate that I was informed by my English professor that I would not be successful in his class or the University because I had come from a predominantly African American high school. This same professor refused to accept my grade after I made a blind copied submission to the English department; scoring the highest out of all entries. His reasoning? Simply that I could not have scored that high considering I was from a school in what he considered the "hood" (my word, his insinuation). Though traumatized by his words, I was determined to prove him wrong and that, I did. Upon successful completion of my program, I invited him to join my proud and loving community to celebrate my success, which he did. Ironically, I returned to this same University when I decided to pursue my doctorate. After all, if I'd done it once under this scrutiny, I could do it again and maybe this time, my experience would be void of judgement based on the color of my skin.

Considering my deeply seated desire to live in community, it came as no surprise that when I made the decision to pursue a doctoral degree, I looked forward to entering a new realm of academics. Maybe, just maybe, I could find the kindred connection which evaded me the first time. My program was a hybrid cohort model, meaning the number of students would be small and our intensives would be just that—intense. Deep within I knew that the number of African Americans would be extremely small simply by virtue of the fact that I was attending a predominantly White institution. This truth, however, actually fueled my belief that there was a high probability that those few of us of the melanin existence, embarking on this trek at this point in time would be more inclined to band together on some level to complete this journey. Real talk? I wanted a "sista" to share this experience with who understood the realness of the struggle and the resulting sweet taste of victory because she was at the table with me. Finally, I would possibly be in community with African American academics with whom I could be unapologetically Black when, and if, I wanted to.

I still recall my first intensive session and introduction to the forced community that I would have to spend the next two years with to successfully complete the program. I could feel the energy of the room as I walked down the hallway and approached the doorway of our first meeting space. It was a mixture of high anxiety and determination manifested by nervous laughter, awkward exchanges of pleasantries, and impulsive attempts to reassure oneself of the ability to be successful through the recitation of resumes to total strangers with hopes that their response would build confidence. I made the decision to stop just within the doorway to take it in, get a lay of the land and, most importantly, scope the room with hopes that I would find someone who looked like me. While my eyes did fall on an African American male who I ultimately developed a great connection with, he was not the Sista I had hoped for. I soon realized that the group which I stood observing was only one of two classes that would afford me the possibility of that seemingly elusive connection. In fact, there was a Sista in the cohort before me. I had high hopes for our ability to have at least an exchange or two on what to expect with words of wisdom culturally hued in a way that would reflect the tongue of my people who had so influenced my life, relax me enough to breathe through the moments ahead and fortify me for those times of depletion which were sure to come. Yeah, no…that didn't happen.

Instead, this hoped-for melanin sibling in the quest for higher academic ground, who would possibly play some role in building me up for the climb ahead, and for whom I was willing to do the same, would not even acknowledge my existence. When I attempted to say hello in passing, I was made to feel like the underclassman who dared to speak to a senior back in high school. Simply stated, how dare I even attempt to align myself with her greatness and academic stature? Once again, my hopes for that Black Girl Magic connection were dashed. By her actions, I was temporarily catapulted back into that mindset that the professor attempted to cloak me in so many years earlier. Namely, I didn't belong and, more impactfully, I would have no allies who looked like me, who would walk with me on what should have been a notorious journey in my life.

Initially hurt and confused by her dismissal, anger and ultimately sadness soon cropped up in my headspace. Reflecting on numerous times in my life when this was my reality, I acknowledged this was not an isolated experience. Why was it a Sista making me feel so small? Why couldn't we support each other as Black women, especially in environments where we were so few? Had I made a mistake by only attending a predominantly White institution during my academic tenure? Had I cheated myself out of a richer tribal experience in exchange for an externally defined "best" that was, in my mind, designed to give me some ill-defined professional edge? Why, on my academic course, did I even have to choose between Black cultural enrichment and what the world defined as "the best"? Would I ever truly find my "sista" within my academic network who would restore my confidence that they do exist along my chosen career path?

To explore answers to these questions, I turned to my mom, the first melanin queen who helped me understand the importance of my village, modeled membership, and taught me the criticality of embracing those right spirited individuals who embraced me. She, of all people, knew how deeply steeped I was in the principles of kindred fellowship that have carried me over time. My mom understood that my academic plight has always been an isolator from my family and friends who have not gone with or before me and, therefore had no context for my pain points. It was my mom, my greatest coach, cheerleader, and critic, who brought me back from the ledge of self-doubt, lurking regret, and cynical stereotypical judgments, which were trying to set up residency. She reminded me that the celebrants of my multiple successes in life were not always kissed by the sun the way we were yet they had all consistently picked me up, pushed me forward, and cheered me on. In her own way, she brought me back to the reality that community, in the fullness of its riches and poverty, is not limited to assumed connection or cultural familiarity that skin color may suggest. Rather, it is that unifying circle of individuals who enrich your life and center your soul through commonly embraced ideals, traditions, and rituals. Finally, she re-instilled in me the understanding that it was the other woman's loss, not mine, considering all I was willing and able to bring to the communal table for her to partake of. Yes, my queen showed up for me by delving into the recesses of my mind and bringing to the forefront what community is all about and who I am as a trusted partaker.

So, during the next intensive when invited to dinner by a group of seniors in celebration of their approaching graduation, I accepted. While these women of varying cultural persuasions poured out their experiences, successes, failures, and words of wisdom, we broke bread through tears and laughter, and I feasted until satisfied. I soaked it all up like cornbread absorbing the flavorful pot liquor from the last of some good collard, mustard, kale, and turnip greens. My palate was refreshed by the tall glass of sweet tea ladled up by unexpected hands. Finally, I'd found communion at a table encompassed by women interested in my journey who did not look like me but, nonetheless, embraced me. Like so often in my life, Mom was right. There were those who wanted to embrace me, whom I chose to embrace back.

That night, my academic community, which feeds me even now, took shape. Unfortunately, missing from the table was another melanin skinned and minded "sista." That absence now fuels my personal vow to avoid perpetuation of this occurrence whenever possible. How? By acknowledging the presence of a fellow "sista" in professional and academic settings even if no more than with a smile and nod of my head to her greatness even if she doesn't recognize it. By making myself available to my "sista" who may be considering pursuing her doctorate but lacking confidence that a brown-skinned girl can persevere considering the culturally hued struggles she has faced. But mostly, by remembering what it felt like to walk into the room and be immediately discounted without cause, particularly by another "sista."

Part III

Race, Space, and Time

Race, Space, and Time accentuates the experiences of doctoral students from their perspective as people of color in predominantly and historically White institutions. Articulated from this perspective are the shared expectations for a better future for the next generation of scholars of color to navigate these spaces. The authors speak directly to the heart of institutions of higher education, and their responsibility to make room and prepare for the fullness of who students of color are. Not simply in outward appearance of diversity, but the scholars in this section charge institutions with keenly examining the ideological concepts of equity and inclusion to operationalize a true appreciation for and support of students of color; emblematize well in these spaces. Further, the narratives here share the interconnectedness of the constructs of race, space, and time to the academic experience.

Race as one construct for defining and identifying the scholars, is discussed as the perpetuation of stereotyped expectations. The concept of space described herein addresses the environmental constitutions which position and engage scholars within a racialized context, and presupposes students of color on the margins. Within the scholars' narratives, time is generative; it is necessary to produce hope, perseverance, and the fortitude that stands in dialectical opposition to the oppressive and racist ways of the academy . Together, the concepts of race, space, and time encapsulated with this section depict the nimble resilience these scholars of color have developed, and the power of their triumph over struggle to define a path for themselves and generations to come.

18 Unmasking Academia for Future Generations

Onda Johnson

The road to doctoral candidacy and a completed dissertation required persistence and evoking a deeper sense of myself. I re-entered graduate school after a significant amount of time had lapsed between completing a master's degree and acceptance to a doctoral program. I was uncertain how this gap in time would impact my ability to keep pace in graduate courses. Looking down the road, I was determined to focus on what laid ahead. I prepared myself mentally for the challenges and refused to look back at what was behind me.

In my experience there had been a slow uptick in education over the 15-year period I was away from higher education. In most courses we sat in rows, in lecture-style classes, using PowerPoint, a technology introduced to me during my master's program more than a decade and a half before. I had envisioned a more progressive space, in the classroom and in higher education.

The curriculum covered in the program was current; the ideologies, perceptions, expectations, and culture remained decades behind. It appeared to me that higher education had been in flux over these years. The university's policy on diversity was slight at the graduate level. The general profile of a graduate student where I attended was White, middle class. Fifteen years before entering the doctoral program, I was one of two African American students in my master's program cohort. The ratios were similar in the doctoral program.

My personal history in education was a mixed bag of unmet expectations and lost potential. I began the doctoral journey with a promise to myself, the commitment to blaze a path for others to follow, and the desire to meet this challenge with a victorious end.

Unlike the trek I suspected other students in the doctoral program had taken, I began my educational career at a local community college. I matriculated to a four-year college to complete an undergraduate degree and years later I completed a master's degree. In between, I raised a family and built a career. Successful navigation through the doctoral program required a deep level of commitment, self-regulation, resilience, and academic acumen. Identifying what Simon Sinek, author, and professor, referred to as your "why" was critical in each stage of the scholastic process. Drawing on what motivated me to pursue an advanced degree provided the foundation to propel me toward the completion of this goal. Along with my faith, it is where I drew my strength to continue through the struggles of self-doubt and self-deprecation.

Preparing for Scholarship

My educational career was filled with negative experiences that were punctuated by discrimination. In this final step of my academic career, I was determined to not allow the negative experiences of the past to define me or my scholarship. I entered the doctoral program on my own terms, diffusing the negative stereotype and diametric self-fulfilling prophetic responses. I would refute the assessment of my academic competence by the teachers and professors of the past and would instead draw on this energy to move beyond the limited expectations that were central in my educational history.

I was prepared to face the pitfalls that had previously caused me to stumble, the academic diversions placed in my path intended to keep me off track. In the beginning the biggest challenge I faced was the pre-recorded messages in my head telling me that I was not worthy, prepared, or suited for this academic challenge. If you ask me what it was like to prepare for the doctoral program, I would say "it was a mental thing."

Developing Scholarship—Building Resilience

The challenge to finally meet my academic potential would be my constant battle—it served as a source of inner strength to defeat the self-induced obstacles produced from the trail of doubt kicked up from the dust of the past.

Distinguishing myself in the classroom meant dispelling stereotypes. I cringed each time I saw the astonished looks on the faces of some of my classmates when I responded in class or at the number of times I heard the "you're so articulate" type comments. I had to learn to brush aside these microaggressions and not allow their generalities about me stifle my scholarly development. Graduate programs carry an air of privilege and elitism, and the environment is highly competitive.

There is a hierarchy, at least in the minds of some of the students, defined by where you completed your undergraduate and graduate degrees. My pedigree was incomparable to most of my classmates, but I understood that it did not matter where I came from, what was important was what was in front of me. For me, the question of where I completed my former degrees was an attempt to discredit my intellect and I would not allow myself to be defamed. I assured myself that the personal sacrifice I was making would count, and I would not be dejected by the attempt to keep me in my place.

I had to commute two-and-a-half hours each way to get to campus. Usually sleep deprived, my days began long before sunrise and ended after sunset. I would watch the sun envelope my car as it rose behind me, chasing away the darkness and pushing me forward. The early mornings usually followed late nights putting the final touches on presentations or papers, skimming the required readings a second time to be prepared for the classroom discussion. Being attentive for eight hours in class on Saturdays or five hours after a full day at work was a task all by itself. But, I did it...praying the whole way!

When asked how things were going during the first phase of the program, I would respond by saying, "I'm handling it!" Understanding the institutional culture and the people you come in contact with is important to fulfilling your goal, it is integral to how you navigate around potential barriers and survive in the process. There will be all types of obstacles: racism, culturalism, and a myriad of biases. So, creating a plan to overcome them is essential to your success— preparation is key.

The Battle Is Won

Persistence has been theorized as a mechanism by which some students find success in educational environments. My journey to a completed dissertation was fraught with many high and low points, frustration, despair, and elation; oftentimes happening in unison. The experience was unmatched in the depth of resolve and fortitude it demanded and the academic challenges it presented. In 2016, the National Center for Educational Statistics estimated that in 2014, the year I began my journey, nearly three million students entered post-baccalaureate programs including: master's, law, medical, dental, and other professional programs. The research on the rates of attrition for graduate students suggested that nearly fifty percent of these students would drop out within the first year. I was resolute in my commitment not to become a part of this statistic.

I entered the institution with a clear set of expectations and values for the type of student I would be and who I would become in this environment. Most importantly, I maintained the posture that I earned the right to hold a position in the student body despite the inequitable education I experienced throughout my educational career.

As a doctoral student in an institution that espouses social justice, I experienced both subtle and outwardly biased behaviors. I was concerned for the sparsity in enrollment of students of color that represented a systemic example of an inconsistency in the institution's diversity policies. In the four years it took to matriculate through the doctoral program, I rarely encountered newly admitted students of color, particularly African American students, a puzzling experience given the proximity of the university to urban neighborhoods.

I had to look past these adverse situations and not allow the social, cultural, and environmental deficiencies of the university to upend my goal to completion. The most salient advice I received about the dissertation, was to choose something that you care about as the topic of your research. The research topic I chose was one I felt would be an important addition to the body of research on African Americans. I tested my research topic through a number of writing assignments in courses leading up to my doctoral candidacy. This approach provided a source of feedback and input that was invaluable when I began shaping my research. It also provided the time to consider the resources, methodologies, and tools that I might use to support the study. Using this method of capacity building kept my focus on my end goal and provided the guideposts and direction for the study.

The arduous process of developing and completing an approved study was infused by my concern for finding study participants. There is a wealth of research available on African Americans. As a subculture, we have been studied in every way possible and most of this research has been produced by individuals that are outsiders to the African American community. As an African American woman, I was particularly interested in representing the narratives of individuals from my community.

I wanted to make a contribution to the research from a different paradigm and point of interest. Doing this research required introspection on my part, I needed to be vulnerable to my potential participants to establish my place in the community. I knew I would have to reveal my connection to their histories in order to gain their trust.

In the end, I was blessed through the stories that were shared with me, the representations were rich, poignant, and varied. The support from the woman in my study enriched my life and provided depth to my study.

Completing a doctoral degree is a significant challenge. It taxes your being in indescribable ways. Garnering the mental and emotional support is just as critical as being prepared academically. Motivation is what will bring you to this stage, persistence will keep you there, perseverance is what is needed to reach this goal.

If asked what it took to complete a doctorate, I would say that it took a lot of prayers, belief in myself, and most importantly, the perseverance to keep moving forward in the face of what appeared to be impossible.

Reference

National Center for Educational Statistics (n.d.). Fast Facts. Retrieved from: https://nces.ed.gov/fastfacts/display.asp?id=27

19 Finding Your Place

Overcoming Imposter Syndrome

Katrina Ramsey Arnold

To the Black woman who is struggling to find her place.

You belong. You are Worthy. You Matter. You are intelligent. You are exactly where you are supposed to be.

Imposter Syndrome is real. According to the experts, Imposter Syndrome is a psychological phenomenon that is common amongst highly successful people. It robs you of your success and regardless of your experience, education, or accolades, Imposter Syndrome embodies you with a sense of unworthiness. When those internal voices tell you that you are not good enough, it weighs on you. You begin to believe it and it is bonded to you, like an unwanted companion that is constantly with you.

When I walked into my very first course in a doctoral program at nearly 30 years old, the fraud associated with this syndrome became even more real to me. I decided to pursue my doctorate after completing a master's degree. I maintained my career as a community college educator while enrolled full-time in a master's program. Working full-time while in graduate school was a challenge, but my work ethic and passion for supporting students at the community college level fueled my desire to do both. I quietly navigated higher education as a student and an employee, and as a result of this experience, I knew that a doctorate was the next step for me.

You Belong

I had every reason to believe that pursuing a doctorate was perfect for me. For as long as I could remember, I had always been told that I was smart. I excelled in school for the most part and even when I struggled, I was always able to finish strong. The same was true in my career. Up until I started the doctoral program, I worked at two community colleges for several years. As a practitioner, my experience in higher education was an attribute. I suspected that my teaching experience would add relevance, credibility, and depth to my input in classroom discussions and in my understanding of theories that supported higher education research. Not to mention, my mom had completed her doctorate and I was destined to one day follow in her footsteps. There was no reason in the entire world for me to doubt my future success, but walking into that classroom on the first day of my doctoral studies changed this entire narrative and challenged my own thoughts and beliefs in myself.

I decided to pursue my doctoral degree at the same predominately White institution (PWI) where I received both an undergraduate and master's degree. As a quiet, small-town girl, it was safe and I was familiar. It was also convenient. I lived in the same town as the university and I only worked 40 minutes away during that time. It was a perfect match, but what I didn't expect was to feel so out of place in this very familiar environment. I felt displaced and unworthy.

The first class was an opportunity to get acquainted with other cohort members, as well as the professor. It also offered an opportunity to dive right into the course itself. I sat quietly in the class and listened to my classmates as they spoke so intelligently about their experiences as administrators and instructors at area community colleges and universities. They seemed to already be familiar with the terminology and higher education jargon the professor used as he presented the introductory material. Many of my classmates were eager to discuss and provide feedback. Me, not so much. The feedback I was getting was in my head as my mind was in conversation with itself. What am I doing here? Should I know what they are talking about? I think I am in over my head. Am I sure that this is for me? As I sat in that classroom, I felt invisible. All of the preparation and experiences that had brought me there meant absolutely nothing. According to me, I did not belong and I possibly needed to rethink my decision to pursue a doctorate.

You Are Worthy

The support of my family and close friends gave me the strength to continue to pursue my doctoral degree. While I left that first class feeling completely out of place, I continued to attend. When I left class each evening, my confidence would return and I would remind myself that I was where I needed to be, that I was smart enough, and that I could one day complete this degree. Even with my confidence restored, when I returned to class, I would again second guess myself.

In class, I was reluctant to share my thoughts and would often sit and listen to my classmates discuss similar ideas that I had, giving me confirmation that I was on par with them, but I was too afraid to speak up.

In my experience, Imposter Syndrome is more significant when you are Black and as a Black woman, it is even worse! When you find yourself in a room filled with people and most of them do not look like you, it is easy for Imposter Syndrome to set in. Black women are constantly reminded by society, and by those who are not Black, that we do not belong in these spaces. Debilitated by racism, discrimination, and microaggressions, their sense of self-worth and value wanes, leaving in its wake feelings of self-loathing and inadequacy. This is how I felt that first year in my doctoral program.

You Matter

I was one of two Black women in my cohort. I distinctly remember one day after class, my professor approached me and asked if everything was okay. I said, "Yes, why do you ask?" He responded by telling me that someone in the class had expressed concern because I was very quiet in class and did not contribute to the discussions as much as everyone else. I could not understand why someone else would be concerned about my classroom participation. Later, I mentioned the conversation to my classmate, the other Black woman, and she told me that the professor had the same discussion with her. I am not sure if this conversation occurred with any others in the class, but I found it interesting that the only two Black women in the class were being questioned.

One piece of advice I have is that establishing relationships with other Black women and students of color in your program is necessary for survival. I realized this following the interaction with my professor. I needed someone to confide in that would understand me and share my concerns and someone I could relate to. I also realized I was not alone in what I was experiencing in this program. What I came to understand was that these feelings of inadequacy were not mine alone, they belonged to many other Black women who were navigating similar spaces.

My time as a doctoral student at a PWI helped me to confront Imposter Syndrome in a way that I had never done before. After that initial year in the program, I realized that I couldn't allow my internal thoughts and societal influences to impact my progression and success. I share my story with other women of color that have similarly recognized this as their own reality.

You Are Exactly Where You Are Supposed to Be

If you are like me, a Black woman in a doctoral program at a PWI, I encourage you, my fellow sister to remain faithful and always believe in yourself. Despite the feelings of unworthiness that may plague or burden you, you must continue to remind yourself that you are intelligent and that you have the credentials and experience to be exactly where you are. Through my own experience as a doctoral student, I was able to develop strategies that helped me to successfully matriculate through my program.

One of the most impactful strategies was developing relationships with other Black women and students of color in doctoral programs. Within my own cohort, I sought out students of color, and I joined a writing group with other Black students, both men and women. There were only a few of us in the cohort, but we bonded through our experiences and were intentional in scheduling time together to write, share, vent, or seek advice from each other. This was exactly the support that I needed to overcome barriers as I progressed through the program. I broadened my access to support by becoming involved in an organization for women of color in the academy. Being a part of this organization cultivated my spirit and helped me to grow. It was encouraging to be around other women of color that were pursuing or who had completed their degrees and were now moving into opportunities in higher education.

The most amazing thing about the relationships that developed during my doctoral studies is that most of these relationships have remained intact post-graduation. Some of my best friends in the academy are those that were there for me through my studies and they continue to support me as I navigate being a Black woman administrator in higher education.

I also leaned on my family for support. I often tell people that my family believed in me more than I believed in myself. I now realize that their belief in me has helped to shape my reality. Sometimes you just need to hear from those that care the most about you. In addition to family, spirituality and a faith system was my guide in navigating through my issues with Imposter Syndrome. In those moments when I wanted to quit, I leaned on my faith to keep me grounded and to guide me through.

Lastly, my work as a community college educator inspired me to push forward. As I interacted with and supported students each day, I knew that I had to continue. I have witnessed firsthand how racially minoritized populations struggle to navigate higher education and successfully complete degrees. In order to have a positive impact on students of color and their growth, I would need to prepare myself for the next level in my career. Completing a doctorate was the first and necessary part of this process.

As I traverse the road ahead of me, I continue to rely on the strategies that I used as a doctoral student. I encourage you, my sister, to own your place. You belong exactly where you are and you are destined for greatness.

20 Who Belongs in Academia?

Jessica Rivera

Growing up I never really knew anyone who had a doctorate. In my predominantly low-income Latinx community in San Antonio, the only people with a college degree were my teachers. Graduation from high school was a major accomplishment in my community. Instead of naming colleges or universities as their next steps, most students "joined the workforce," a clear indicator that our schools were not preparing us for spots at top tier institutions, but rather funneling us into the service industry. Most teachers did not believe that college was a realistic goal for students. Often White teachers or teachers from more materially privileged backgrounds taught at our district knowing they could get away with putting little effort into teaching.

Despite the lack of preparation to succeed in college, I was able to attend a predominantly White institution (PWI) in the Midwestern part of the United States. However, attending this college limited my access to scholars and faculty of color. At this institution, the majority of the people were White and from more privileged backgrounds. It was at this institution that as a master's student I began to entertain the idea of continuing my education after meeting Latinx doctoral students. However, I had an image ingrained in my mind that doctoral students were perfect, type-A students who had this educational trajectory figured out from birth.

Although I did not think that I was among this elite group, I remained curious. As I navigated this idea. I approached a Latina doctoral student to solicit her opinion on my thoughts about doctoral students, instead of demystifying what I understood, she agreed that most doctoral students fit my concept of type-A. Her comments reinforced that I was not PhD material, and it really bothered me that I was right in my self-perception.

What was more upsetting for me was that I actually believed this narrative, I recall thinking, how could another student of color make me believe this? Being in a doctoral program made me realize that the power structures at play had convinced her that there was only room for so many Latinx students in doctoral programs. I interpret this as an example of the ways in which dominant power structures manifest themselves to make people of color feel like they need to compete with each other. It may be that some people feel so oppressed, that being one of a few makes you feel exceptional in some way—special in a way that makes it seem like you were able to overcome oppressions that maybe others were unable to.

For many years I doubted whether I was PhD material. In addition to not being a type-A student, after completing a master's degree I still felt unprepared for a doctoral program. I took a detour and went into teaching, but there was a small part of me that still wanted to pursue a PhD. I was between moving home and staying in Wisconsin, when I reached out to a Latina professor. She encouraged me to focus on pursuing a PhD and highlighted assets that uniquely suited me for a doctorate.

Honestly, at that point, I was still not convinced. After teaching for three years I moved on to a position at a Hispanic-Serving Institution (HSI). I was fortunate enough to be working alongside amazing Latina mentors. My new boss, a first-generation college student with a similar background to mine, had just earned a doctorate. She supported my growth and helped me gain the confidence to enter a doctoral program.

Working at an HSI was different from the university where I previously attended and was employed. In the common areas you could hear music in Spanish, Latinx art covered campus walls, and there was a noticeable presence of diversity in the faculty, staff, and administrators. I received the mentorship and guidance from my supervisors, they helped demystify the doctoral experience, and constantly reminded me that I was PhD material. What I understood from these individuals was the narrative I held close—that I was not PhD material—existed in higher education to keep certain people out. Events on this campus also played a major role in my decision. One evening I attended a panel of first-generation faculty. A Latina professor shared the numerous barriers she had overcome, barriers that made my life seem like a walk in the park. The stories I heard resonated with me and made me realize that I too had a place in academia. Collectively, the messages I received while working at an HSI helped propel me to apply to PhD programs.

My Doctoral Experience

I was not prepared for what was in store for me. Being in a doctoral program will completely change your world. You will gain a critical lens that becomes incredibly difficult to turn off. You will no longer be able to just sit through a movie without critically analyzing it. Everything you watch to some extent is under examination and general conversations at times become challenging. As a Latina, it was challenging, especially being at a PWI in the Midwest. Fighting racism, sexism, and classism was a constant.

During my first year, I was the only Latina in the majority of my courses. My first semester was plagued with microaggressions and being tokenized as the only Latina in the classroom. The irony was not lost on me that my fellow students, who had been studying the impact of racism, were untouched by what they had learned. I was working with a group on a presentation about race, when a White student shared that she thought it would be great to discuss microaggressions in our presentation. She looked at me and asked, "Maria what do you think?" I'm not sure why she called me Maria when my name is Jessica, I was so shocked by what she said that I did not know how to respond. I concluded that, often, people in academia have intellectualized concepts like racism to the extent that they block out the real life application of what they have learned.

Most of my energy was spent educating my White, privileged classmates about the experiences of minoritized people. It was clear that this limited experience with someone different from them would not erase what they believed, and in some ways it had exacerbated their racist comments.

Straddling Different Worlds

I struggled with survivor's guilt: the guilty feeling a person gets when they feel they survived a difficult situation that others did not. I first experienced survivor's guilt when I was accepted in the doctoral program and I was told how lucky I should feel to have this opportunity. I remember thinking that I didn't want to feel lucky. I didn't want to be an outlier in my community. Why was it that I was lucky, while others weren't? It should be the norm that people of color are able to pursue their dreams. As a doctoral student I constantly felt guilty that others in my community are not in the room with me.

I straddled several worlds. While on campus I lived in a middle class, White community During breaks I would return home to a low-income, Latinx community in San Antonio. It was not uncommon to see people in their seventies or older waiting for the bus with their lunch bags in hand on their way to work. This was in stark contrast to the people that lived in Wisconsin, where I attended college. There the people I would encounter who were over 65 years old, would be wearing workout clothing for walking around the neighborhood during the day, enjoying their retirement. Retirement for many in my community at home rarely exists even in my own home; neither of my parents will have a retirement check waiting for them when they stop working.

Class became an even more salient part of my identity. Most of my peers do not understand what it is like to come from poverty and experience the firsthand struggles associated with that. On campus, middle class perspectives on access dismisses issues such as not having the funding to attend a conference, missing the opportunity to present your research. Being in a doctoral program creates the narrative that academic attainment defines and adds value to a person. This ideology is at odds with the people I value at home and in my community.

Resisting Challenges

The challenges continued into the selection of a dissertation topic. I sat down with two people from my cohort to narrow down our dissertation topics. I explained to my peers the paralyzing pressure I felt to come up with an amazing topic. As a woman of color I am already perceived as unqualified in this space. However, I feel an obligation to write something that will support my community. The pressure to produce research that will have significance to my community only makes the process more challenging. As I explained this to my peers, the response from one was a total shock. As a White man, my colleague could essentially write about whatever topic he wanted, without the potential for scrutiny. I expected to face a lot of scrutiny in electing to focus my research on the Latinx community.

At times I think of how liberating it would be to not feel the added pressures. Talking to friends and faculty who are invested in my success has helped me navigate these issues. Many of us who come from marginalized communities have been exposed to narratives that hinder our success. As I entered my doctoral program I hustled to find a community because I knew this process would not be easy. This has allowed me to find great mentors in fellow graduate students, faculty, and staff.

A Message to Future Doctoral Students

As I think back, I wonder what response I would give if a student today asked me, "Do you have to be a type-A person to be in a PhD program?" I would share that while it may seem like the majority of doctoral students are type-A, that is only one side of the story. There are many narratives that make us believe that we are unworthy. There is nothing wrong with or lacking in you. I am not type-A and I do not come from privilege, but that does not mean that I am not PhD material.

Throughout the doctoral program, I faced the pressure to fit into stereotypical patterns in denial of my true self. I advise you not to fall into that dominant ideology to make others comfortable with you. Instead, focus on the way you would prefer to show up, speaking your mind, being a leader. While I faced more challenges in an institution that was not designed for me, I did not internalize that deficiency. Academia will need to embrace those who do not fit the "norm" of a scholar.

Tension in institutional settings is a catalyst to stretch beyond the breaking point and to force change. The change that is needed in academia is not in me, it is in the culture of the institution. Unraveling the racial and cultural biases in higher education will stress a system that has normalized my discomfort. The evidence of progress will be when higher education adjusts its lens to see people like me and you in these academic spaces.

21 An EdD in a PhD World

Developing a Scholarly Identity in a World That May Not Always Recognize You as Legitimate

Erin Doran

Deciding on a Program

As an undergraduate and master's student in history, I originally wanted a PhD in that field with the goal of becoming a tenure-track faculty member. After graduating with my master's degree in 2008, I worked full-time, taught at the local community college, and learned languages I would need in the field of history. Some hesitation hit me when a series of articles in the *Chronicle of Higher Education* spelled out the unwelcomed reality that job prospects for PhDs in history were terrible.

Like others, I feel like I fell into higher education, and I didn't realize that I had found a career after my master's. I was an academic affairs professional at the University of Texas at San Antonio (UTSA; also my alma mater), and I was moonlighting as a history instructor at a local community college. It was my side hustle that made me fall in love with community colleges, so I ultimately decided to find a doctoral program that would keep me engaged with the kind of work I was doing as a young professional, and that would enable me to move up the chain of command through higher-level administration.

The Realities of My Doctoral Choice

In 2009 and 2010 as I was thinking about doctoral studies, I was the main breadwinner for my partner and me at a time when the country was still in the middle of the Great Recession. My partner, who studied to be a high school social studies teacher, struggled to find a job because nearly every district in our area went on a hiring freeze or had so few jobs open due to declining retirements. In thinking through higher education-related programs, I thought about other programs in the area, including a PhD at the more prestigious University of

Texas at Austin. However, having to commute more than 50 miles each way would have either required me to quit my job (when I was the source of medical insurance for both of us) or spend a substantial portion of my paycheck on gas at a time when gas prices had risen significantly. In the end, I decided to stay local enough that I was attending courses in the same building where I worked full-time. I've been very honest when I tell people I didn't choose UTSA; I chose to pursue a doctoral degree at the university where I happened to work. That enabled me to keep my benefits, to contribute to my household program, and to take advantage of my tuition benefits so I could avoid taking out loans for my doctorate.

Re-Negotiating the Scholar in Me

I entered the EdD (Doctorate of Education) program in Educational Leadership in 2011 at UTSA. I also assumed that my changing fields, my aspirations of the tenure-track were done. As a result, I also did not give much thought to the fact that the program I decided to pursue was a Doctor of Education program instead of a PhD, a degree that is often perceived as a "PhD-lite" or a watered-down doctoral degree. I assumed all that mattered was that I was getting a doctorate. I found that within the first year, the inclination to conduct research and to keep my options open for a faculty position post-graduation were strong. With mentoring from my advisors, the recommendation was made to me to have two book reviews and two manuscripts under review before I graduated. The convenience of being on the same campus (even the same building) as my doctoral program enabled me to finish before most full-time students.

In reflecting on my experiences, I do not feel that pursuing or having an EdD *always* mattered, but there were key moments when I felt some of others' (mis)conceptions of what an EdD is or should be.

"EdD Programs Are Not as Rigorous as PhD Programs"

Part of my full-time position when I was in my program was to recruit doctoral students for a PhD program in teacher education. The program often attracted prospective students who were deciding between this program and the K-12 Leadership emphasis of the EdD in Educational Leadership. It was not uncommon for students to ask what the differences were between the programs and the degrees themselves. In one particular information session, a faculty member interrupted me as I was about to respond to the difference between an EdD and PhD, and he said, "EdD programs are not as rigorous as PhD programs." He went on to say that most EdD programs did not require as many research methodology hours nor did they require dissertations. In the case of the programs at our university, not only did the EdD program require the same number of minimum hours in research methods as the PhD program, the faculty in the EdD program carried most of the burden of offering and teaching research methodology to students in the PhD program.

I remember feeling demeaned by this man's words and worrying that no matter what I did, he would never view my degree as the same as his. It took multiple years for me to understand that he had no power over my choices or career trajectory, so whatever he thought about the value of my degree meant nothing in reality. But I can't say it didn't hurt, and I have talked to many EdD students and graduates since this happened who share a similar story.

"The PhD Graduates Get Everything—Including the Jobs"

The above faculty member's perception about EdD programs was not an isolated encounter for me. I made the choice early that when I would get described as a "PhD student" in introductions or in public spaces, I would clarify that I was an EdD student to ensure that no one thought I was misrepresenting myself in any way. While on the job market and in conference spaces, imposter syndrome around my degree and where I went to school crept in. I applied for so many tenure-track jobs, including jobs at institutions that were at-level with UTSA in terms of size and reputation. Over multiple application cycles, it was hard not to notice that I was often not getting past the phone interview or that jobs were being filled by graduates of some of the most prestigious institutions— the University of Texas at Austin, UCLA, Michigan, and so forth. When I lost out on a job for which I had the only campus visit to a UCLA graduate, I was devastated. I was at least still employed full-time by UTSA, but I was in a job that I had long outgrown and was looking for the next opportunity. Like many doctoral graduates, I felt like all I needed was someone who could give me a chance.

I won a dissertation award from the Council for the Study of Community Colleges in 2016 that I still say changed my life. About a month later, I received a call from Iowa State University asking if I was interested in interviewing for a Visiting Assistant Professor position. I interviewed and received a job offer quickly, which I accepted.

I moved to Ames, Iowa sight unseen with the understanding that there would be a tenure-track job opening for which I was eligible to apply. When I made it to the on-campus interview round, my feelings of inadequacy crept in as I watched graduates from Michigan and other equally reputable institutions come to Ames for their campus visits. Soon, I accepted a tenure-track job offer on February 14, 2017, something I consider a Valentine's Day gift to myself.

"I Don't Get to See Many Faculty Who Have EdDs"

In Fall 2018, I received a direct message on Twitter from a woman of color who followed me and lived in the Midwest. She asked if we could meet sometime during the Association for the Study of Higher Education (ASHE) conference in Tampa, Florida, without giving me much reason why she wanted to meet. I assumed it was related to my institution's ongoing faculty search. Early on in the conversation, she shared with me that she was a current EdD student, and she asked to meet with me because she had not encountered any other ASHE attendees who were either pursuing an EdD or held one. She eventually ended the conversation with gratitude, saying "I don't get to see many faculty members who have EdDs." This exchange influenced me to look specifically at the credentials of teaching faculty in EdD programs and to see what proportion of EdD faculty hold these degrees themselves.

"Let Your Work Speak for Itself"

Oftentimes, I find myself going back to the words of one of my mentors, an EdD graduate who is now a Full Professor at large, public research university. She continually reminded me that when you do good work—whether that be in scholarship or in practice—the work will eventually speak for itself. Another EdD graduate, and friend, also told me that she had to sometimes remind herself to "keep my eyes on [my] own paper." My reality has been that when you give in to insecurity and imposter syndrome, it psychs you out. It keeps you from believing in yourself. It makes you believe that you're not capable or don't deserve a seat at the table, wherever that may be.

Concluding Thoughts

Something that I may not have been as explicit about to this point is that I identify as Latina. Anecdotally, so many of the EdD students who I interact with at conferences or on Twitter are people of color themselves. I still have yet to find the data to support my guess that people of color are more likely to be in EdD programs than elite PhDs, but I do know that we may choose these programs because we can't sacrifice a full-time paycheck or have our basic needs met as a full-time PhD student. That does not make our experiences and knowledge any less valid. To people of color in EdD programs, I offer two things: First, own your knowledge, your voice, and your contribution. Write about it, present it, tell about it on social media. Higher education needs your perspective more than it will ever admit. Second, *write, not right.* This was shared with me by a Black male educator who taught writing at the community college where I taught. He was telling me that I could always fix my ideas and make them more academic—but first, I had to get them down. The first draft doesn't matter.

To members of search committees, I beg you: Give EdD applicants a chance. You may find that they have more wealth in lived experiences, experiential knowledge, and a tenacity that can't be taught. EdD students may have been perfectly capable PhD students in other circumstances, but they had families to care for and bills that needed to be paid.

In the end, I knew that my work would ultimately speak for itself, but I also needed someone to give me a chance.

22 Hope as Praxis, Pedagogy, and Purpose

Using a Critical Post-Traumatic Growth a Framework to Navigate Traumatic Environments

Stacey Chimimba Ault

I had a lot of insecurity about entering a doctoral program. I dropped out of high school in my teens, and rushed through my early college years with a vendetta to prove everyone wrong. I no longer carried rageful energy. Left behind was imposter syndrome and an abundance of fear. I realized, in order to be truly successful, all the parts of my identity (teen parent, high school dropout, Black immigrant, prison wife, community advocate, school district leader) would have to become visible. Throughout my life, I had battled racism, poverty, intimate partner violence, and exploitation. I kept most of my lived experiences hidden. Life for many survivors is often covered in a deeply rooted sense of shame. Inherently, I knew graduate school was going to be the place where I desquamated the layers that protected me, in order to truly expose myself in a way that could facilitate change.

I was a single parent of six and guardian to two additional teenagers, my younger brother and my daughter's best friend. This of course, added an additional layer of complexity to my decision to return to school. I was unsure how I would manage parenting, education, my career, and my deep commitment and engagement with young people. I also wrestled with the paradox of being in the academy as opposed to being in the community. I wondered if it made sense for me to take time away from the direct advocacy work that was so critical to spend time theorizing in a classroom.

Ultimately, I went to school anyway even though many of my fears and questions were not necessarily resolved; and even though I was afraid, graduate school gave me the academic language I needed to implement sustainable change-making strategies within my community. It also allowed me the space to learn about, and with, social justice and human rights scholars who themselves were deeply engaged in the community. It afforded me a lens into work that pushed my boundaries and connected me more deeply to the work that is my life's work. I gave myself permission to lean into my organic relationships with youth and community through learning about participatory action research and community engaged scholarship.

My doctoral research was a Youth Participatory Action Research (YPAR) project that also included an examination of my own experiences with trauma and growth. Making my research personal allowed me to develop deeper relationships and push back on the narrative that research is something that takes place in a sterile environment without personal bias or reflection. I wanted to add to the body of research that considered how the juxtapositions of trauma and growth played out in the life of the young people I conducted research with. I subsequently developed the conceptual framework of Critical Post-Traumatic Growth (CPTG), and used this framework as the methodological and theoretical framework for my dissertation. I use CPTG as a method to investigate my own doctoral experience, to make sense of the trauma and growth I experienced while in my program, and to reflect on how doctoral students can examine their trauma and growth using this lens.

Critical Post-Traumatic Growth

This theory was conceived within a YPAR project I conducted with Black female high school students. I constructed CPTG to offer an alternative framework to examine the trauma, wellness, and growth for ourselves and our students as persons of color. Current trauma narratives paint a solely deficit-based view of trauma that never fully explained my lived experience, or the experiences of the youth researchers and participants.

When I share my story with people, they often feel compassion for the traumatic experiences I have been through, but fail to acknowledge how global systems of colonialism and oppression have directly impacted my existence. Furthermore, when I share my successes, people attribute them to my own resilience and applaud me for being so strong. However, as McGhee and Stovall assert in their 2015 article about how racism hurts black college students, individuals are often drawn to an emotional response without a deep examination of how this harmful narrative does not recognize the stress and strain associated with academic success amidst racist policies and educational practices, nor does it account for the toll societal racism has on Black students.

As doctoral students, I encourage you to lean into the theorizing space. When I conducted my dissertation proposal defense, the biggest takeaway from my committee (aside from the statement that my literature review reminded them of a very long book report) was that the theoretical frameworks I was pulling from did not fully provide a thorough line that I could use to pull each area of my dissertation together. I embraced the opportunity to produce new knowledge once I realized that I could create a conceptual framework that didn't merely explain the literature, or justify my research topic. As a result, this new approach framed each phase of my project, including my methodology.

Critical Post-Traumatic Growth Praxis

I offer CPTG as a framework in this time through which you can examine the experiences of others, but also a lens through which you can acknowledge your own trauma and inspire personal and collective growth. The tenets of CPTG are context, suffering, identity, community, navigation, resistance, voice, and hope. By exploring these tenets in my research I was able to further the conversation about how educational spaces at all levels can be sites of trauma. In the same manner the tenets of CPTG can also be used to develop a blueprint for students and educators of color to grow. My praxis of CPTG unfolded as I worked in concert with youth in my community.

Context: It refers to a critical analysis, and understanding, of the spaces within which we exist. We should examine and name the social or institutionally engineered trauma we are experiencing. While my doctoral program was rooted in social justice and Critical Race Theory, racism still surfaced, generally in the form of microaggressions and lack of, or push back on, culturally relevant support for myself and other Black women in the program.

Suffering: Secondary trauma occurs when we witness others experiencing trauma. During my graduate program several students were killed in our community. The youth I interacted with seemed to be dealing with death, or the fear of death, on a regular basis. They also battled undiagnosed mental health issues, self-medicating, homelessness, sexual abuse, assault, and incarcerated family members. Their suffering could not be minimized nor the impact it had on me while on my own educational journey and the research I was conducting. After a bloody weekend of over fifteen shootings,and police presence in our community I and other adult allies met with the young people in our lives to encourage, listen, share space, and breathe peace.

Identity: Traumatic experiences, inside and outside of school, resulted in me asking myself why I even chose graduate school in the first place. I leaned on my own strong ethnic identity in order to counteract the feeling of invisibility and mental and physical extermination that I experienced and witnessed. I made sure to bring my authentic self to the classroom to engage with and challenge the curriculum in creative ways, even if this meant tears and frustration. Our positive ethnic identity correlates with how we navigate racialized spaces.

Community: I brought my community with me and I encourage you to bring your community with you. Say their names. With permission, share their stories. Force people to look at them, see them, know them. Your classmates will likely be leaders and decision makers someday. Make sure they leave knowing a little bit more about your community. Leave a mark on them so they are encouraged to do no harm, and use their privilege for good. As members of the school community, you can also hold people accountable when they are dishonorable. Also develop your own community within your program. Even if you are introverted and afraid (like me) the relationships you make will be an important source of support.

Voice: As you become more comfortable sharing your voice, be aware of trauma porn. Sometimes people are fascinated with stories of death and grief and trauma. For some people, they just can't look away; but they don't really "see" either. Be careful that when you speak your truth you don't sacrifice yourself. The emotional labor of being the only person of color in the classroom is real. Recognize the trauma in this. Also, remember your unique why. Whatever the reason that brought you to graduate school, remember that. Write it down somewhere. As much as you may hate reflection journals, they may be a space where you can share your authentic voice. Of course, your own journaling practice can also be effective as you process your trauma.

Resistance: As a graduate student examine your own experience and locate any trauma triggers. These triggers may be contextual or interpersonal. Take individual or collective action in order to minimize the impact of trauma. Active ways of coping, such as explicitly naming and confronting racialized microaggressions are shown to alleviate the stress of these incidents. Your very existence in these spaces is resistance. I wanted to earn my doctorate to prove to myself that even though I made a lot of mistakes, I still had an opportunity to fight for my own freedom. Even though I dropped out of high school, I could still earn the highest degree attainable. I resisted the narrative that uplifted my "resilience" and "success" and rather used this space to create a battle plan that moved us toward a more liberatory environment for all.

Navigation: As we learn to navigate educational spaces, our work must make space to confront trauma and to consider strategies for resistance. While in school, a professor forced me to face my own compassion fatigue, and inspired me to have more authentic conversations with the class. The next class I held a healing circle. Implementing educational transformation means we must integrate a philosophy and world-view of well-being, healing, and joy into our daily practices. You may find you need more in depth clinical support as you move through trauma to growth. Don't be afraid to go to therapy or work with a coach, during or after graduate school. Remember, graduate school is traumatic; you will need time to detox and process.

Hope: Amidst the context of oppression and suffering I experienced more than a few glimmers of hope. Black women (and people of color more globally) wrapped around each other and reminded ourselves regularly of the importance of healing justice, self-care, and squad care. I bore witness to radical academics building authentic relationships with youth resulting in deeper community engaged scholarship. I engaged in YPAR methodologies that minimized othering, and placed young people as producers of knowledge. Both myself and the students experienced individual and collective growth. As a scholar of color your very completion of this process is advocacy. Share your work, use your voice, your participation gives us hope.

Finally, adopt a pedagogy of love. This means loving yourself, your community, your family, your dissertation, the process, and etc. This courageous love also brings hope to others. Love is an act of courage, not of fear, love is commitment to others. It is the process of loving yourself enough to look fear in the face and keep going. You got this.

Epilogue

Dear friends and colleagues,

The question of whose knowledge should take center stage and what comprises intelligence and scholarship is at the crux of the issue that students of color encounter in the American educational system. By choosing what is central to the discourse, who is teaching, what is being taught and how it is being taught, educational systems maintain a new type of asphyxiation by determining priorities that either exclude or minimize the history, struggle, and accomplishments of people of color. Therefore, the pursuit of education is a political act not unlike other movements or uprisings of past generations.

This book was written at a time when the American society was grappling with episodes of anti-Black violence and widespread injustice. Mourning the deaths of Ahmaud Arbery, Breonna Taylor, and George Floyd, and enraged at the victimization of Christian Cooper and so many others who stood against longstanding and grave injustices of racism, we wept, held spaces for reflection, protested and asked ourselves, "what's next?"

Although the world battled a health pandemic, which disproportionately affected Black and Brown communities and highlighted healthcare disparities, people of color continued to battle the world's "isms" which oscillate to maintain power and keep us off-kilter. We understand that every time the wound of racism is exposed again by senseless acts such as the murder of an unarmed Black man and the portrayal of undocumented individuals as criminals, it further compounds the inhumane experiences that people of color have.

Exigent circumstances like these require a response and often mandate that people of color choose which life to save: physical, emotional, spiritual, or material. All of these lives are essential in living our best life, but we are often forced to sacrifice one to save the other. There are so many others whose stories have not been catapulted into

National and International headlines or whose daily struggles have been all but forgotten. The various accounts in the preceding chapters are a barometer for the ways in which people of color are still being maligned, discounted, tortured, overlooked, and assassinated by the academy—but not without hope, community, and realizing great achievements.

During this epoch of social unrest when anti-Blackness is at the forefront of the nation's pandemic manifestations, this volume serves as an artifact that describes the state of the academy for people of color during an era that has been touted as a "Post Racial State" and an environment in which we are assumed to be free from racial preference, discrimination, and prejudice. We mark this moment in time—this work—as a response to the call of those who have bled and died before us to RISE UP. We too are reaching out to you and encouraging you to join the fight, do your part to go down in history as a contributor to the change that is to come.

In solidarity & power,
Emerald, Bridget, & Onda
Co-Editors
Elevating Marginalized Voices in Academe

References

Gutiérrez y Muhs, G. (2012). *Presumed incompetent: The intersections of race and class for women in academia.* Boulder, CO: University Press of Colorado.

Hill-Collins, P. (2000). *Black feminist thought: Knowledge, consciousness, and the politics of empowerment.* New York: Routledge

Hooks, B. (1994). Teaching to transgress: Education as the practice of freedom. New York: Routledge

Kena, G., Hussar, W., McFarland, J., de Brey, C., Musu-Gillette, L., Wang, X. ... Dunlop Velez, E. (2016). *The condition of education 2016* (NCES 2016-144). Washington, DC: U.S. Department of Education, National Center for Education Statistics. Retrieved April 22, 2019, from http://nces.ed.gov/pubsearc

Kennedy, D. H., Terrell, S. R., & Lohle, M. (2015). A grounded theory of persistence in a limited-residency doctoral program. *The Qualitative Reporter, 20*(3), 215–230.

Kuntz, A. M. (2015). *The responsible methodologist: Inquiry, truth-telling, and social justice.* Walnut Creek, CA: Left Coast Press, Inc.

Ladson-Billings, G., & Tate, W. F. (1995). Toward a critical race theory of education. *Teachers College Record, 97,* 47–68.

Lewis, C. W., Ginsberg, R., Davies, T., & Smith, K. (2004). The experiences of African American Ph.D. students at a predominantly White Carnegie I-research institution. *College Student Journal, 38*(2), 231–245.

Lorde, A. (1988). *A burst of light: Essays.* Dover Publications: Mineola, NY

Nash, R. J. (2004). *Liberating scholarly writing: The power of personal narrative.* New York, NY: Teachers College Press.

National Center for Educational Statistics (n.d.). Fast Facts. Retrieved from: https://nces.ed.gov/fastfacts/display.asp?id=27

Solorzano, D. G., & Yosso, T. J. (2002). Critical race methodology: Counter-storytelling as an analytical framework for education research. *Qualitative Inquiry, 8*(1), 23–44.

Tuck, E. (2009). Suspending damage: A letter to communities. *Harvard Educational Review, 79*(3), 409–428.

About the Editors

The editors are all qualitative researchers whose backgrounds are diverse and in many cases are interdisciplinary. Their experience and extensive networks provide a web of access to individuals and groups who are often relegated to society's intersectional margins.

The editors are each well-qualified to lead this project and to discuss the sensitive nature of writings about personal experiences. As qualitative researchers, counseling professionals, and persons who have attained high security and confidentiality clearances they have conducted focus groups and interviews regularly. They know the value of an uninterrupted story and are disciplined in maintaining the integrity of the speakers words. Not only have each of them experienced traversing the doctoral journey as persons of color in a historically White institution, they have worked in different industries that traditionally have been predominantly White and male (Education, Law Enforcement, and Local Government) in which they have served as educators, supervisors, and directors. One with a background in counseling, is skilled in establishing rapport, unconditional positive regard, and goal setting. Another has experience in making complex decisions regarding hiring and coaching employees, while managing a high level of security clearance within their organization. And, still, the other has many years of experience creating and defining educational strategy for Kindergarten-12 grades at the State level.

The editors are well accomplished, their intent is to provide a counter space where people of color can interact with a variety of contributors to share common experiences in a nurturing and encouraging way. Readers will be strengthened by the stories of challenge and triumph amid resources and tools. At least two of the editors published in scholarly journals that address the continued need for social justice advocacy in our Nation.

Emerald Templeton, EdD

Emerald Templeton has an expertise in higher education and student affairs. Her publications include peer-reviewed articles and a book chapter in the Career Planning and Adult Development Journal, Journal Committed to Social Change on Race and Ethnicity (JCSCORE), and the Association of Mexican American Educators (AMAE) Journal. In 2018, she earned her doctorate from the University of San Francisco in Organization and Leadership. She has presented on issues related to practice and research in higher education at conferences for: American Counseling Association (ACA), American Educational Research Association (AERA), Association for the Study of Higher Education (ASHE), Student Affairs Professionals in Higher Education (NASPA), and National Conference on Race and Ethnicity in American Higher Education (NCORE).

Bridget Love, EdD

Bridget Love holds dual roles: an administrator in a local government agency, and a professor of communication studies. An intercultural communication specialist, Dr. Love is a community educator/activist with a lifetime of lived experiences as an African American woman navigating white spaces. Her publications include peer-reviewed articles in the Journal Committed to Social Change on Race and Ethnicity (JCSCORE), and the International Journal of Qualitative Studies in Education (QSE). In 2017, she earned her doctorate from the University of San Francisco in International and Multicultural Education. Her research is centered on creating spaces of dialog where African American women can curate, custodian, and produce their own identity using narrative, community, and art as vehicles to share commonalities, explore truth, remove lies, and promote equity. She has presented on issues related to the marginalization of Black women, and equity and inclusion in higher education at the following annual conferences: Hawaii International Conference on Education (HICE) and National Conference on Race and Ethnicity in American Higher Education (NCORE).

Onda Johnson, EdD

Onda Johnson is an Education Administrator in the California Department of Education. A specialist in the development of educational programs, Dr. Johnson has worked with students with severe educational challenges to meet their educational goals. Earning her doctorate in 2018, in Organization and Leadership from the University of San, her research is focused on the process of single African American mothers to engage educational institutions to support their son's academic development. Her research focuses on the intersection of the identity, role, and the experiences of African American mothers to navigate educational spaces.

Contributing Authors

Ms. Jasmine Abukar
Jasmine Abukar is an educational equity advocate, facilitator, and PhD student at The Ohio State University. Her academic specialization is in Multicultural and Equity Studies in Education, where she pays attention to how students with marginalized identities formally and informally resist oppression within higher education. This research focus is inspired by the scholarship of feminists of color, historical, and contemporary activist movements on college campuses, and her own experiences as a first-generation college graduate and Woman of Color with disabilities. A native of Connecticut, she identifies strongly with her East Coast and Black Latina roots. In her free time, she's an avid sports fan, reader, music lover, and wellness evangelist.

Ms. Stephanie Aguilar-Smith
Stephanie Aguilar-Smith is a cisgender Latina, bad bruja scholar, and wife. She is a first-generation Venezuelan immigrant, naturalized US citizen, and first-generation graduate student educated and employed at all predominantly White institutions. Raised in a blended, middle-class family, she is the youngest of six children. With this upbringing, Aguilar-Smith's research interests include the evolving profile of Hispanic-Serving Institutions, the relationship between public policy and organizational strategizing, and inclusive praxis within academe. Tying all her work together is her organizational and policy bent and her commitment to challenging systemic, structural inequities perpetuating the marginalization of long underserved communities. Currently, Aguilar-Smith is a PhD candidate in Higher, Adult, and Lifelong Education, jointly pursuing a certificate in Chicanx/Latinx Studies, at Michigan State University. Aguilar-Smith earned her Master's in Public Administration with a specialization

in Higher Education Administration, a B.A. in Journalism (Public Relations), and a B.A. in International Affairs from the University of Georgia.

Dr. Stacey Chimimba Ault

Dr. Stacey Chimimba Ault is an Assistant Professor in the Social Work Division at Sacramento State University. She is a healer, activist, scholar, leader, and mama, to her biological children and the young people in her community. Dr. Ault's scholarship revolves around Critical Post-Traumatic Growth among individuals and communities, as well as examinations of Blackness and anti-Blackness in communities and institutions. She conducts participatory action research alongside youth and community in order to effect change. Her dissertation was entitled, Queens Speak: Exploring Critical Post-Traumatic Growth among Black female students in the school to prison pipeline.

Dr. Ault has over 25 years' experience working with children and families in the Sacramento area. In 2016, Dr. Ault founded the Race and Gender Equity Project. Their mission is to harness individual and collective transformation through healing, education, advocacy, and research.

Mr. Ivan Carbajal

Iván is a doctoral candidate in Behavioral Science. He studies the interplay of culture and neuroscience, investigating the emerging field of Cultural Neuroscience. His dissertation focuses on the unique processes of code switching in bicultural and bilingual Latinxs and its effects on visual recognition. Iván identifies as a bicultural, bilingual, queer, first-generation Mestizo Mexican-American. His upbringing as a son of Mexican immigrants in a conservative area of West Texas has shaped his worldview and has initiated many journeys exploring racial, ethnic, cultural, gender, and sexual identity within not only himself but also his community. Iván hopes to build a career out of being himself and following his passions, wherever those may take him.

Dr. Ashley Carpenter

Dr. Ashley Carpenter is the UCEM Program and Diversity Initiatives Coordinator within the Office of Graduate Education at Massachusetts Institute of Technology. In these roles, she helps coordinate several initiatives that attempt to increase the recruitment of diverse students, support student research and success, improve retention and time to degree, and create more cohesive for underrepresented and underserved communities. Furthermore, her passion for diversity and inclusion in higher education is rooted in her research, which explores the ways minoritized students use their cultural capital to successfully transition from high school to college. As the examination of culture and identities are pertinent to her academic and professional career, her positionalities impact her work. Ashley Carpenter is a Black, middle-class, cis-gender woman from Chicago. Dr. Carpenter is a lover, a researcher, and an educator who attempts to make educational spaces more equitable for people that look like her.

Dr. Latoya Council

LaToya, a Black Feminist Scholar Activist is an expert on work-family conflict and its intersection with health and well-being for Black American middle-class individuals. LaToya's dissertation entitled, "Her Work, His Work, Their Work: Time and Self-Care in Black Middle-Class Couples" interrogates how Black couples manage work and family demands with individual self-care practices. In 2017, LaToya co-founded her company, CLC Collective LLC where she currently serves as the Chief Academic Officer. The mission of CLC Collective is to create awareness and action around issues regarding diversity and inclusion for children through the incorporation of intersectionality. CLC wrote their first children's book Intersection Allies: We Make Room for All published by Dottir Press. LaToya says, "intersectionality and the power of love frames how I view the world and my place within it."

Dr. Erin Doran

Erin Doran is an Assistant Professor of Higher Education and Community College Leadership at Iowa State University. Erin completed her EdD at the University of Texas at San Antonio (UTSA) in Educational Leadership in 2015. Her dissertation on developmental education reform in Texas received the Dissertation of the Year Award from the Council for the Study of Community Colleges in 2016. Her research agenda encompasses three areas: Latinx college students, especially those placed in developmental education; the faculty who teach these students; and the Hispanic-Serving and Hispanic-enrolling institutions where these students attend. Erin is a multi-ethnic cis-gender female who identifies as Latina and White. She grew up on the Texas-Mexico border in El Paso, Texas.

Dr. Linda Garrett

Linda Garrett is a graduate from the University of San Francisco, where she received her doctorate in International and Multicultural Education. She has over 20 years' experience working with faith-based organizations to build capacity and better serve the people. Linda is a qualitative researcher, with expertise in document review, document analysis, and the evaluation/exploration of historical artifacts. She is also a craftivist who combines her activism with a love of crafts, in order to engage in, and teach, critical self-care. Dr. Garrett also has over a decade of experience working for the State of California in varying capacities.

Ms. Kayon Hall
Kayon Hall is a foreign-born Black woman and PhD Candidate in the Higher, Adult, and Lifelong Education (HALE) program at Michigan State University. Through the use of critical theoretical and methodological approaches, Kayon's research focuses on Black immigrant students, diversity and social justice, and anti-Black racism in higher ed.

Ms. Angel M. Jones
Angel Jones is a doctoral candidate at George Washington University. Her research is grounded in Critical Race Theory and focuses on how the racialized experiences of Black college students affect their mental health. Her research interests include racial microaggressions, racial battle fatigue, gendered-racism, and counter-storytelling. Her dissertation explores how Black graduate women respond to, and cope with, gendered-racial microaggressions at a historically White institution. She identifies as a Black and Latina woman, as well as a first-generation college student.

Mr. Jesse Moland, Jr.
Jesse Moland, Jr. has nearly 20 years of experience in K-12 education. A Black male with a background in computer engineering, he served as a teacher, teaching physics and pre-calculus, and the director of technology. After earning his master's degree, he became an assistant principal while remaining in the classroom part-time. Now, as a doctoral candidate studying higher education administration at Oral Roberts University, he is interested in the role that the digital divide plays in the continuance of educational inequalities. His dissertation is a hermeneutic phenomenology examining the perceptions of first-year college students' experiences with the digital divide in public schools.

Dr. Angelina Nortey
Angelina is a licensed psychologist in the District of Columbia Metropolitan area (DMV). Her specialization is youth mental health and integration of culturally responsive practice and social justice principles in clinical work. She also serves in roles such as school-based team

manager, supervisor, and adjunct professor. Angelina's family is from Ghana, West Africa and identifies as Black/Ghanaian-American. This identity strongly shapes the ways in which she views the world and helps her to maintain a global perspective and understanding. She was born in New York City and raised in the suburbs. Angelina identifies as a non-(dis)abled heterosexual woman.

Dr. Verna Orr

Verna Orr Verna holds a PhD in Higher Education from the University of Illinois at Urbana-Champaign and is a three-time graduate of Howard University. Currently, she serves as a Post-Doctoral Research Associate at the National Institute for Learning Outcomes Assessment. She has served as a school administrator for Washington, DC Public Schools and Confidential Assistant to the 16th President of Howard University. Verna is a co-founder and co-chair of the Historically Black College and University Collaborative for Excellence in Educational Quality Assurance (HBCU-CEEQA). Verna's research interests include assessment, accountability, access, equity, student learning outcomes, and HBCUs.

Ms. Mignon Page-Broughton

Mignon Page-Broughton is an agent of social justice. She has twenty-eight years of family service experience and continues to focus on the entire family through the lifespan. Currently, Mignon serves as a Deputy Probation Officer. She has assisted with the creation and implementation of prevention programs throughout the peninsula in Northern California, and works alongside youth in the community to design programming. Previously, she provided intensive case management to youth with significant pathology and family challenges. Her research interests include higher education accessibility, educational motivation among adolescents, and psychosocial factors related to juvenile delinquency and education. She holds a bachelor's degree in Child and Adolescent Development from San Francisco State University and a Master of Science in Clinical Psychology from Notre Dame de Namur University. She has completed her doctoral work, and is currently writing her dissertation.

Dr. Janise Parker

Janise Parker is an Assistant Professor of School Psychology at William & Mary. She is a licensed psychologist and a nationally certified school psychologist. Her research focuses on culturally responsive practice in school psychology and school-based mental health support.

Dr. Parker was born and raised in the Southeast. She identifies as an African American, non-(dis)abled heterosexual female, who is deeply connected to her Christian faith.

Dr. Lisa J. Price

Lisa J. Price, a proud African American woman, daughter, mother, sister, and friend, completed her Doctorate of Nursing Practice in Executive Leadership at the University of San Francisco. With a particular interest in end-of-life care for African Americans and clinician cultural competence, Lisa's doctoral focus challenged clinicians by exploring their personal biases, stereotypes, and prejudices that interfere with promoting an optimally trusting healthcare encounter among this underserved population. Through the development of interactive workshops designed to present the experience of African Americans within the continuum of care from slavery to the present day, participants expanded their foundational understanding of medical mistrust, damaging historical events, and the resulting relationship between healthcare providers and the African American community.

Lisa has been an invited lecturer on topics such as transformational leadership, complex adaptive systems, fiscal stewardship in the face of declining reimbursement and hospice philosophy and regulatory compliance. With a career spanning over 25 years, Lisa has been privileged to care for individuals and families facing life limiting diseases while serving teams in various leadership roles. Currently, she is a Regional Director of Hospice for one of the largest healthcare organizations in the United States.

Dr. Katrina Ramsey Arnold

Dr. Katrina Ramsey Arnold completed her Doctorate of Education in Educational Leadership – Higher Education Administration degree in 2017 from East Carolina University. She is a proud Black woman who has a passion for education and supporting students as they pursue higher education. Dr. Arnold's research interests include community college leadership, Black women leaders and their experiences as administrators at community colleges, and supporting students of color at community colleges. Dr. Arnold is currently employed as a community college administrator and is extremely active in her local community. She is a member of Alpha Kappa Alpha Sorority, Inc. and the National Council of Negro women. She also volunteers her time with local non-profit organizations. Dr. Arnold currently resides in Greenville, NC with her husband and daughter.

Ms. Jessica Rivera

Jessica was born and raised in San Antonio Texas to immigrant parents from Mexico. As a child, she entered the educational system in the United States only knowing Spanish. The community she grew up in was made up of mostly low-income Mexican families. After graduating from high school, Jessica decided to attend college out of state at the University of Wisconsin-Madison. The transition to college was a difficult one as a first-generation college student attending a university that was drastically different from the community she came from. Five years later Jessica graduated with an undergraduate degree in art, and later completed a master's degree in educational leadership. Over the past ten years since graduating from college, Jessica worked at different educational institutions, as an admissions counselor, an academic advisor, a third-grade teacher, a program coordinator promoting Latinx student success as well as a supervisor for peer-mentors in a first year experience program. All of these experiences led her to pursue a doctoral degree in higher education to continue her efforts in promoting the academic achievement of underrepresented and minoritized students and dismantling the power structures that impede their success.

Dr. Christy Wynn Moland

Dr. Christy Wynn Moland completed her Doctoral studies at Louisiana State University in Baton Rouge, LA. Dr. Wynn Moland is an adjunct assistant professor and licensed and nationally certified speech-language pathologist. She also served as Director of Clinical Education of a university Speech and Hearing Clinic. Her research interests include child language acquisition, screening, and assessment in linguistically diverse populations.

Index